13.4.15

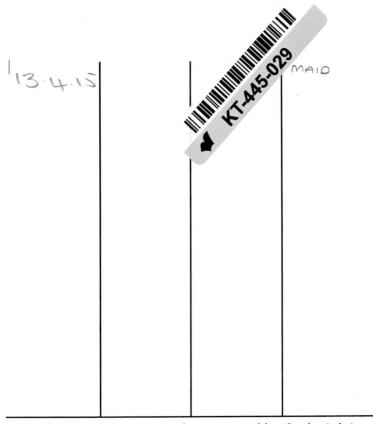

KT-445-029 MAID

Books should be returned or renewed by the last date above. Renew by phone **08458 247 200** or online *www.kent.gov.uk/libs*

HOMEWORK
HELP
for
MUMS
and
DADS

HOMEWORK HELP for MUMS and DADS

HELP YOUR CHILD SUCCEED

Karen Dolby

Michael O'Mara Books Limited

First published in Great Britain in 2011 by
Michael O'Mara Books Limited
9 Lion Yard
Tremadoc Road
London SW4 7NQ

A CIP catalogue record for this book is available from the British Library.

Papers used by Michael O'Mara Books Limited are natural, recyclable
products made from wood grown in sustainable forests. The
manufacturing processes conform to the environmental regulations of
the country of origin.

ISBN: 978-1-84317-490-5

1 2 3 4 5 6 7 8 9 10

www.mombooks.com

Illustrations by David Woodroffe
Designed and typeset by D23

Printed and bound in Great Britain by Clays Ltd, St Ives plc

CONTENTS

Introduction

How many parents can honestly say that their heart hasn't sunk on occasion when their child comes home from school and greets them with the words, 'I've got homework. Can you help me?'

This seems to be especially true of maths, or numeracy, as it's more often called today. Many parents freely admit maths was a subject they loathed at school and left gleefully behind at the earliest opportunity. Homework is one part of childhood that no one remembers fondly, and not many people relish doing it over again. At the same time, however, we all want to help our own children and would hate to think they were losing out or lagging behind at school because of our lack of know-how and support.

A common complaint from parents is that teaching methods and vocabulary have changed immeasurably since their own schooldays, leaving them floundering and with the distinct impression that their 'help' has simply caused more confusion and problems.

Homework Help for Mums and Dads aims to supply you with everything you need to know to usefully help your child – not by doing the work for them, but by offering valuable support and practical guidance. It covers everything from how to establish good homework habits and create the right work environment for your child to useful tips from other parents and teachers. It looks at all the main subjects taught in your child's early years at school, including the all-important maths and literacy, as well as helping them prepare for their continuing education.

Each chapter approaches its subject in a way that is designed to be most helpful, so the chapter on Numeracy contains fun number games, while the one on Science suggests easy experiments you can try at home. There are also tried-and-tested memory tricks and clear guidance on problem solving. I hope to remind you of things you used to know and explain others that are completely new to you. Most importantly, I hope to give you ideas on how to pass your knowledge on to your children whilst making learning fun in the process.

One
Homework Habits

'Education is the best provision for old age,'
ARISTOTLE

Homework is as much about developing good home-working habits as the work itself, especially in the early years at school. Like it or not, homework is a big part of school and you can make a real difference just by being on hand. There are no hard and fast rules that work for all children, but there are some simple steps you can take to make life easier.

- Provide somewhere inviting for your child to work. A desk, comfy chair and light in a child's bedroom are always a good idea, but you may find your child prefers to work somewhere near you. The kitchen table often seems to be a favourite, which is fine as long as you can keep distractions to a minimum.
- Try to set a routine for homework that suits everyone. It may be that your child likes to complete any work as soon as he or she gets home, but children are often hungry after school so a snack and drink first can be a good idea. You may even find that they work better after some time out relaxing or playing.
- Developing a set after-school routine means everyone knows what's expected. This can be especially helpful later at secondary school when homework becomes more serious.
- Avoid starting homework too late in the evening; children find it harder to concentrate when they are tired.

- Few children are keen on homework, so try not to worry that you have the only reluctant child.
- It can be hard balancing the needs of different-aged children but try not to let younger siblings flaunt their free time too much.
- Check that children know what their homework is when they come out of school, and that they have everything they need before going home.
- Most schools now give out homework diaries – if not, encourage your child to keep his/her own.
- Encourage your child to plan ahead for homework. Children are often given several days to complete a task and it's tempting to leave it to the last minute, overlooking evenings when they are busy with something else.
- When children find it hard to concentrate, it can help to split homework into shorter sections with a break in between. Give them a timer or a clock so they can chart their own progress and feel in control.
- If you see your child's attention wandering, take an interest in what they are doing. Look at their books and ask what question they are working on.
- Encourage research. Make sure children know how to find out information for themselves – from books, libraries and the Internet. The web in particular offers great scope for fact-finding but children need to be aware that not all websites are always accurate.
- Encourage children to read through their completed homework. It is very useful for children to get into the habit of checking their own work.

PARENTS' TIPS

DON'T:
- Allow homework in front of the TV – it's never a good idea.
- Do the homework for them.

DO:
- Offer children something to look forward to once the homework is done – it could be a game of football or time on their games console, a favourite TV programme, or even a sleepover with a friend.
- Give help and advice, or sit with your child while they are working, particularly if they are finding something difficult. Always praise the positive before you point out any mistakes.

How much homework should I expect?

UK government guidelines are clearly set out, emphasizing that homework should help children learn and reinforce lessons taught in the classroom. These guide times are suggested:

> *Years 1 and 2 – one hour of homework each week.*
> *Years 3 and 4 – one-and-a-half hours each week.*
> *Years 5 and 6 – thirty minutes per day.*
> *Years 7 and 8 – forty-five to ninety minutes per day.*

Obviously, some children work faster than others and will complete set tasks in less time. Homework will not always be written work and this is especially so for younger years – it may be reading, games to practise maths skills, or finding information.

Schools are generally happy for parents to support and even help younger children with homework, but as children get older it is important for them to work independently and show what they have learned on their own.

TEACHERS SAY

If you find your child is really struggling with a particular piece of work or topic, do speak to their teacher or write a note explaining they needed a lot of support. That way the teacher can offer extra help and will not wrongly assume this is something your child understands. It can be useful to check with your child's school exactly what is expected of them and how long homework should take.

Two
Numeracy

*'[Never] confess that you don't understand their
maths homework,'*
MIMI SPENCER, THE TIMES

Modern Maths

The most important change to maths at school – apart from
the fact that lessons are now called numeracy – is the focus.
For instance, most parents were simply taught a method and
shown how to divide or multiply, whereas children today are
encouraged to learn why a method works, to understand the
maths behind a problem. In theory, this should build greater
number sense and the confidence to tackle more complex
maths.

Not everyone agrees that the newer methods are always
better, but if that is the way your child is being taught then it
is really important for you to follow that method. To attempt
to introduce your own tried and tested formula will more than
likely lead to confusion and misery on both sides. The most
important thing you can do as a parent is to boost your child's
confidence – and especially with maths, many problems
simply arise from a fear of failure and lack of confidence.

HELPFUL HINTS

- Find out how your child's school teaches a topic.
- Read any textbooks or source material carefully before you attempt to help.
- Sometimes it is just a question of helping your child understand what their homework is actually asking them to do.
- Try not to get discouraged and always give positive feedback. Never get frustrated or annoyed.
- Encourage your child's school to offer parents' sessions to explain current teaching methods.

Mathematical Vocabulary

The vocabulary can be one of the most daunting aspects of maths homework for parents. At first sight, there appears to be a great deal of jargon and confusing technical terms, some of which may be completely new to you, others you may have simply forgotten from your own schooldays. It can seem like a foreign language but understanding just a few key terms can really make a difference.

Here is a checklist of some of the most common:

Angles – an **acute angle** measures less than 90º; an **obtuse angle** is greater than 90º but less than 180º; a **reflex angle** is bigger than 180º; and a **right angle** is 90º. Two lines at right

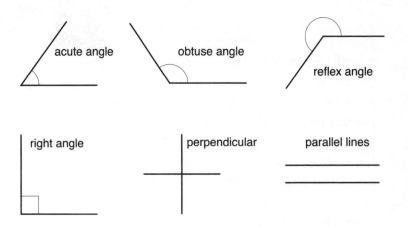

angles to one another are **perpendicular**, while two lines running alongside each other that never meet are **parallel**.

Array – this refers to a set of numbers, shapes or letters set out in a rectangle, and used in schools to demonstrate multiplication and fractions. An everyday example would be a window with three panes across and four down. It is 3 x 4 but if you turn it around it is also 4 x 3, which both make 12.

Breadth, width and length – breadth and width are the same thing and usually refer to the shorter side of a shape. Length is the longer side.

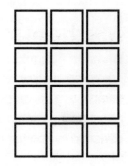

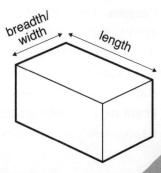

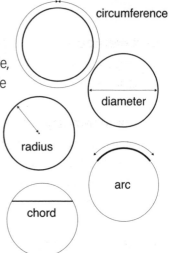

Circles – the **circumference** is the measurement around the circle, the **diameter** or width of the circle is the line across the middle; the **radius** is the distance from the centre point to the edge and is always half the diameter. An **arc** is a small section of the outer edge, and a **chord** is a straight line across the circle that does not go through the centre.

Compensation – in maths this is when you simplify a sum by rounding a number up or down to make it easier. For example, adding 300 instead of 291 and then compensating at the end by taking away 9 from the answer.

Division – **chunking** means to group chunks of the dividing number or **divisor** and subtract them from the **dividend** (the number you are dividing up). The answer in a division sum is called the **quotient**. You may also be asked if a number is **divisible** by another number, for instance, is 24 divisible by 3?

Factors – are all the whole numbers that divide exactly into another number. If you are asked to **factorize**, you are being asked to find all the factors of a number. **Prime factors** are factors that are also prime numbers.

Fractions – the **numerator** is the top number and the **denominator** is the bottom one.

Grid method – this is a way of teaching multiplication by drawing a grid and is often the first step towards teaching long multiplication (see page 42).

Line of symmetry – is the real or imaginary line through a symmetrical shape which divides it in two, with both parts exactly mirroring each other.

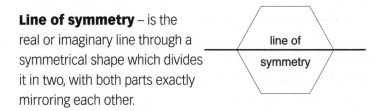

Mean – is the average found by adding everything and then dividing the total by the number in the group, so the average of 9, 5 and 4 is 6.

Median – is also an average, or more exactly the number in the middle in a range of statistics. The median can often be a more useful number than the mean, as outlying numbers (one or two much lower or higher numbers) can skew results. For example, if a class's maths test results were typically 16, 17 or 18 out of 20, the median would be within this range, discounting the one person who scored only 2.

Mode – in a range of results, the mode is the one that occurs most frequently (see TEACHERS SAY on page 18).

Multiplication bonds – this is another term for any of the pairs in the times tables.

TEACHERS SAY

To help distinguish between different sorts of average, remember mean is the mean one because you have to add up lots of numbers and then divide them. Mode is the modish or fashionable one as it is the most common.

Number bonds – are all the pairs of numbers that add up to the number you are looking at.

Number lines – are used to help with adding and subtracting. They are lines with numbers written beneath them (see page 34).

Partitioning – this is a very important concept in schools today and essentially means to sort numbers into more easily managed groups of 100s, 10s and units. It's commonly used in addition, subtraction and multiplication to simplify sums.

Pi π – 3.1415926 is the unique number found by dividing the circumference by the diameter of a circle. A simple mnemonic sentence can help you remember it, just count the number of letters in each word: 'May I have a large container of coffee.' Or try this limerick to remind you how to calculate the circumference of a circle, as well as pi:

> *If you cross a circle with a line*
> *Which hits the centre and runs from spine to spine*

And the line's length is C
The circumference will be C
Times 3.14159.

Circle calculations – These are the three main equations, or formulas, for circles:

Area = pi X radius squared **or** πr^2

Circumference = pi X diameter **or** $c = \pi d$ **or** $c = 2\pi r$

Diameter = 2 X radius **or** $d = {}^2r$

Did you know?

Pi is a mathematical constant also known as Archimedes' Constant. The ancient Greek mathematician Archimedes was the first to calculate the value of pi to within 0.001 of the exact answer, as long ago as the third century BC. The Greek letter π – spelled out as pi – comes from the Greek word for perimeter. Pi is used in many important formulae in science and engineering, as well as maths.

Fun with Pi

Play a game using a string to measure different-sized circles and their diameters. Whatever the size, if you divide the circumference length by the diameter, you should always come up with pi or a number around 3.

Prime numbers – are whole numbers which can be divided only by themselves and the number 1. Counting the letters in each word in the following sentence gives you the first seven prime numbers: 'In the early morning astronomers spiritualized nonmathematicians.'

2   3   5   7   11   13   17

Did you know?

The one-hundredth prime number is 541 and the one-thousandth is 7,919.

Non-prime numbers are called **composite numbers**.

Test yourself

See how many different ways you can make 30 by adding only prime numbers.

Product – is another way of saying multiply.

Ratio – a relative measure of one thing in proportion to another, e.g. the ratio of girls to boys in the class is 2:3.

Square numbers and square root – to square a number you multiply it by itself, for instance 8 squared is 64 and the square root of 64 is 8. It is also useful to know that **cubic** or **cube numbers** are the result of multiplying a number by itself three times, for example:

$$1 \times 1 \times 1 = 1$$
$$2 \times 2 \times 2 = 8$$
$$3 \times 3 \times 3 = 27$$

Square numbers 1 to 100

If you know your square numbers, it makes finding the square root much easier and the good thing is they follow a pleasing mathematical pattern:

Square No.	Square Root	
1	•	•
(+3)		
4	••	::
(+5)		
9	•••	:::
(+7)		
16	••••	::::
(+9)		
25	•••••	:::::
(+11)		
36	••••••	::::::
(+13)		
49	•••••••	:::::::
(+15)		
64	••••••••	::::::::
(+17)		
81	•••••••••	:::::::::
(+19)		
100	••••••••••	::::::::::

TEACHERS SAY

If you look at the Multiplication Times Table on page 37, you will see that the square numbers run in a diagonal line across the middle of the grid. They occur so frequently in maths that they are worth learning as early as possible.

Sum – this is the total you get when you add two numbers.

Triangles – **equilateral triangles** have three equal sides and three equal angles; in **scalene triangles** all three sides are different lengths; **right-angled triangles** have one angle of 90°; and **isosceles triangles** have two equal sides and therefore two equal angles. Angles in all types of triangle always add up to 180°.

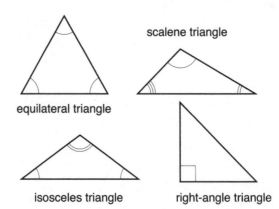

scalene triangle

equilateral triangle

isosceles triangle

right-angle triangle

Everyday Maths

Making maths a part of your normal everyday life is a simple way to help children have fun with numbers without any pressure. Once you start looking, you will be surprised at how many opportunities there are to practise numbers.

Out shopping

- Whenever possible, let your child count out the change.
- Encourage children to help you work out what the items you are buying will come to and check whether you have enough money to pay for them all.

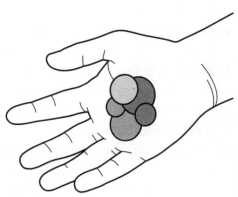

- Standing in the supermarket checkout queue, make a game of estimating how much the shopping will cost. See who comes the closest.
- How much should you estimate each item costs in order to give the most accurate answer?
- Count the number of apples (or another fruit or vegetable) in a kilo. How many apples will there be for each member of your family?

Walking along the street

- Look at the numbers on the houses. For example, do the numbers go up in twos?
- Which are the odd numbers and which are the even?
- Ask number questions such as if 7 X 8 = 56, what does 8 X 7 =?. It may come as a surprise but often, younger children don't make those connections as easily as you'd think. Encourage your child to watch out for number patterns.
- Look at the numbers on the front of buses. For instance, you could watch out for prime numbers.
- At the station, if a train is due in 6 minutes and it is now 11.45 a.m., ask your child to work out what time the train will arrive.

Train timetables

Train timetables are now readily available on the Internet. Ask your child to help you plan an outing. If you need to arrive or leave at a particular time, what train should you take? How long does it take you to reach the station? So what time will you need to leave the house? Questions like these often feature in tests and if children have done the exercise for real, they will not find the problem so daunting.

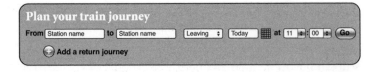

Plan your train journey
From [Station name] to [Station name] [Leaving ÷] [Today] at [11 ◆]:[00 ◆] (Go)
⊕ Add a return journey

Cooking with children

- Baking provides a fun activity with lots of informal number play.
- When weighing and measuring, old-style weighing scales – where you balance ingredients against weights – are particularly useful.
- Compare size to weight ratios with different ingredients.
- Use measuring jugs with different scales for comparison.

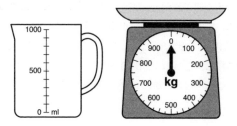

- Ask questions about cooking temperatures and times. For example, how long does it take for roast potatoes to cook at 180°C? What about at 220°C?
- Use a timer to practise subtraction. Casually ask how many minutes have passed, if there are say 7 minutes to go and the total cooking time is 25 minutes.
- Use muffin or bun tins for multiplication. If there are three rows of four, how many cake cases will you need?
- Work with ratios by looking at recipes. If the ingredients listed are for two people, how much will you need to feed four? What about six?
- Children love to help. Ask questions aloud as if you are trying to work out the answer for yourself.

PARENTS' TIP

Once your child is answering your number questions easily, boost their maths' confidence by pointing out the connection with school maths. If they can work it out in a game or everyday situation, then they can also do it in lessons.

In the home

- Use everyday household items to help practise maths.
- Kitchen clocks with clear number displays help children tell the time.
- If there is also a digital clock on a radio or another appliance nearby, they can compare analogue and digital ways of telling the time. In this way, they can also become familiar with the idea of the 24-hour clock.

- Outdoor thermometers are useful as they show minus numbers.
- Calculators are obviously needed for some homework but they can also be used to play calculator games, which can be helpful in familiarizing children with their use.
- Help children gain confidence by checking their maths answers against a calculator.

- The most up-to-date calculators now have fraction functions, although these are not usually used in schools until secondary level.
- Involve children when you are measuring anything using a tape measure – calculating the fabric needed for curtains, for example, where you need to double the window width.
- Squared bars of chocolate, beans, grapes, pasta shapes and coins are all ideal for clearly demonstrating what happens when you add, subtract, multiply and divide.

- Height charts are an excellent way of allowing children to work out how much they have grown over a period of time. They can also look at their siblings' and parents' heights and make comparisons.
- Looking at heights, weights, and even shoe or clothes sizes in different metric systems, all encourage easy confidence and familiarity with numbers in the world.
- Talk about the most appropriate measures for different things. For instance: millimetres for the diameter of a button; metres for the length of a garden wall; and kilometres for the journey to school.

Telling the time

Many children find learning to tell the time very difficult. It's often not something that is taught at school and after a certain age children can be embarrassed to admit they still can't do it. Play/pretend clocks can be very helpful tools. Help them practise by timing homework – if they start at a particular time and work for 20 minutes, what time will it be when they finish?

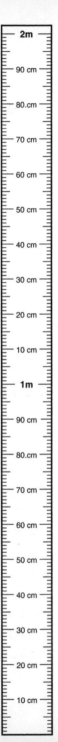

PARENTS' TIP

Try to connect maths to your child's particular area of interest. For instance, football scores and league tables, geographical statistics, proportions and measurements in art, or rhythm and counting in music. Some children like an element of competition – quick-fire contests and star charts can all work, providing they remain fun and not scary. You know your own child so play to their strengths.

Calendar facts

Maths questions often assume a basic knowledge of the yearly calendar. Make sure your child knows the number of days in a week, a month, a year and how

JANUARY

SUNDAY	MONDAY	TUESDAY	WEDNESDAY	THURSDAY	FRIDAY	SATURDAY
1	2	3	4	5	6	7
8	9	10	11	12	13	14
15	16	17	18	19	20	21
22	23	24	25	26	27	28
29	30	31				

a leap year works. Also teach them the order of days and months.

Have a clearly set-out calendar on display, and encourage children to write important dates and appointments on it.

Remember the number of days in each month by the old rhyme:

> *30 days hath September,*
> *April, June and November.*
> *All the rest have 31,*
> *except February alone,*
> *which has 28 days clear*
> *and 29 in each leap year.*

Children also enjoy using their hands. Leaving out the thumbs, tap the knuckles and spaces between them, saying the months as you go along – with January high, February low, March high, April low and so on. When you finish with July high, begin on the second hand with August high, September low until you reach December high. All the high knuckle months have 31 days.

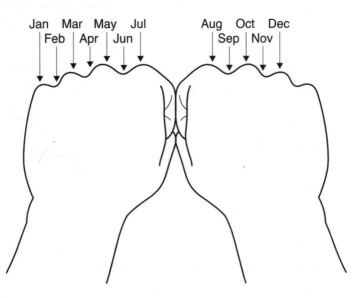

Fun and games

Games are an excellent way to practise maths at home without it seeming like work. Card games, anything using a dice (or even better two!), dominoes, and board games where there is money in the bank, all include counting, sorting, probabilities and chance. Monopoly, Masterpiece and Pay Day have an obvious maths content but if you think about it, even basic games such as Snakes and Ladders require you to roll a dice and count, whilst something like Rush Hour with cars on a grid involves puzzle-solving and patterns, and card games such as whist revolve around probability. Puzzle books and Sudoku, which children can try alone or with you, also encourage number play and confidence.

Number trickery – This is a simple trick to impress your children and help convince them you really do know your maths!

Ask them to pick any three-figure number with three different digits. Next ask them to turn it around and subtract the smaller number from the bigger one, telling you the first digit in the answer.

If it's 9, the answer is 99. Otherwise, you can quickly work it out. The first and last number will always add up to 9, and the middle number will always be 9.

Examples:	902	100
	− 209	− 001
	= 693	= 99

Another trick using the number 9 leaves a little more to chance but it is always fun to try. Without telling you their choice, ask your child to think of any number between 2 and 10. Multiply by 9, then add the two digits of the answer together and subtract 5.

At this point, they will always be left with 4. This is because if you multiply any number up to 10 by 9, the digits in the answer will always add up to 9 – at the end children can check this for themselves.

Again without telling you their answer, ask children to assign a letter to their number, A = 1, B = 2, C = 3 and D = 4, etc., then think of a country in Europe that begins with that letter. The usual choice for 'D' is Denmark, although occasionally people pick Deutschland. Next, they should think of an animal which begins with the last letter of their country – kangaroo is the most common – and finally a colour which begins with the last letter of their animal.

At this point, they will hopefully be amazed when you ask if they are thinking of an orange kangaroo from Denmark, and if that fails, an amber koala, or if they are likely to have opted for Deutschland, a green dog. Even if you're not quite right the first time, this prompts lively speculation about how you know, as well as lots of number play.

Remember

The numbers on the opposite sides of a dice always add up to 7. You can turn this into a game by appearing to guess the hidden bottom number on a dice before letting children into the secret so they can work out the answer, too.

Double dice – Children will happily practise their two times table without even realizing, if you simply let them double any dice number they throw spurred on by the prospect of moving further with each turn.

PARENTS' TIP

Be relaxed about numbers and maths in general. Don't be afraid to ask questions you don't know the answer to. When working something out, allow your child to beat you in the calculations sometimes and to feel they are helping you.

Number challenge – Try to make all the numbers between 1 and 100 using the digits 1, 2, 3 and 4. You must use all four digits but play with them in as many ways as you can, and add, subtract, multiply and divide.

To help get you started with 1:

$$12 \div 4 = 3 \div 3 = 1$$

Adding and Subtracting

Schools still teach the standard techniques for adding and subtracting in vertical sums that most parents remember from their own schooldays, but there is now an emphasis on learning mental methods first. This is to encourage children to understand and make sense of the maths involved, rather than just concentrating on the digits. Number bonds, number lines and partitioning are all key terms.

Number bonds

These are pairs of digits that make up each number, for example 5 is: 2 + 3, 4 + 1 and also 0 + 5. It is very useful to know the number bonds for every number up to 10.

Some children grasp this idea quickly; for others, it can help to use counters or beans so they can literally see how the pairs and numbers work. An old-style abacus is also excellent for this.

Once children realize all the different ways in which a number can be made up, they will already have a good understanding of addition and it will then be easy to introduce the idea of subtraction.

Number lines

Number lines are also intended to help with adding and subtracting, encouraging children with the key realization that if they are adding 7 and 3, for example, then they can count on from 7 and don't have to begin at 1. This would be shown on a number line with an arrow starting at 7 and adding 3 to make 10.

When asked to add or subtract larger numbers, children will then go on to imagine empty number lines for their calculations.

Partitioning

As numbers in sums get larger, it helps to sort them into 100s, 10s and units, and move along the number line by that amount. Most adults do this automatically without calling it partitioning.

Addition is really a continuation of counting but subtraction can be much trickier for children to grasp. It helps to remember all the different ways in which subtraction can be expressed.

Subtraction is 8 – 2, 8 minus 2 or 8 take away 2.

You may also be asked how much bigger is 8 than 2, or how much smaller than 8 is 2? Or, what is the difference between 8 and 2?

When schools first introduce vertical sums, they are often written out to make the 100s, 10s and units clear. Here is an example:

```
      534   becomes   500  30  4
    –  47            – 100  40  7
```

As this still has the trickier problem of taking the larger 40 from 30 and 7 from 4, it can be further partitioned:

```
      400  120  14
    – 100   40   7
```

TEACHERS SAY

It's often possible to turn a maths question into a picture. This can really help children visualize and understand a problem. Children often have no problem with sums if they mean something to them, rather than just being abstract numbers.

PARENTS' TIP

There is not always enough practice time at school. It can be useful to have a workbook to make sure your child is in fact familiar with a topic. You can buy workbooks but there are also many resources and worksheets available to download online.

Negative numbers

The best way to help children understand the concept of negative numbers is to show them an outdoor thermometer with its vertical number line including zero. Some lifts also have one or two floors below ground level, which can also illustrate how negative numbers work.

TEACHERS SAY

Avoid calling negative numbers 'minus' as this can create confusion, since children may think of subtracting instead.

Try playing around with negative and positive numbers to boost familiarity and confidence:

$$-5 \times -3 = 15$$
$$5 \times 3 = 5 + 3 = 8$$
$$-5 - 3 = -8$$

Times Tables

A good knowledge of the times tables is at the foundation of many basic maths calculations at school and throughout life. Children can find learning them a daunting task and it's no less difficult for parents trying to help. Don't despair, there are some simple tricks and short cuts to make them easier.

Multiplication table

Drawing up a multiplication table is a good place to start and a helpful quick reference when needed:

	1	2	3	4	5	6	7	8	9	10	11	12
1	1	2	3	4	5	6	7	8	9	10	11	12
2	2	4	6	8	10	12	14	16	18	20	22	24
3	3	6	9	12	15	18	21	24	27	30	33	36
4	4	8	12	16	20	24	28	32	36	40	44	48
5	5	10	15	20	25	30	35	40	45	50	55	60
6	6	12	18	24	30	36	42	48	54	60	66	72
7	7	14	21	28	35	42	49	56	63	70	77	84
8	8	16	24	32	40	48	56	64	72	80	88	96
9	9	18	27	36	45	54	63	72	81	90	99	108
10	10	20	30	40	50	60	70	80	90	100	110	120
11	11	22	33	44	55	66	77	88	99	110	121	132
12	12	24	36	48	60	72	84	96	108	120	132	144

The best order for learning tables

Start with the easiest, rather than learning them in order:

- **Tens** – the simplest of all. Take the number you are multiplying by and add a zero.
- **Fives** – half of ten and ends alternately in 0 or 5. You can also use your fingers to help.
- **Twos** – double the number you are multiplying by. From a young age most children are comfortable with the idea of doubling, pairs and even numbers.
- **Fours** – simply double the twos.
- **Eights** – double the fours. Beginning with 8, the units descend in 2s throughout the table: 8, 16, 24, 32, 40, 48.
- **Nines** – there are several definite patterns. As the 10s go up, the units go down: 9, 18, 27, 36; the 10s number is always one less than the number you are multiplying by: 9 X 2 = 18, 3 x 9 = 27, 4 x 9 = 36 and so on; if you add the digits together they always make 9 with the exception of 99: 1 + 8, 2 + 7, 3 + 6. There's also a nifty finger trick (see opposite).
- **Threes** – the digits always add up to 3 or are a multiple of 3.
- **Sixes** – when multiplying 6 by an even number the answer will end in the same digit: 6 X 2 = 12, 6 X 4 = 24, 6 X 6 = 36, 6 X 8 = 48.
- **Elevens** – this is easy if you remember to put the two digits of the number you are multiplying by together: 22, 33, 44.
- **Twelves** – by now the only new number you need to learn is 12 X 12 = 144.
- **Sevens** – always one of the trickiest but following this order of learning means the answers have been covered already by the other tables.

PARENTS' TIPS

- Think of alternative ways to teach something that is difficult. 7 X 8 often causes problems. Think 5, 6, 7, 8 or 56 = 7 X 8.
- Make sure your child realizes that if they know 3 X 8 = 24, they also know the answer to 8 X 3, 24 divided by 8, and 24 divided by 3.

Nifty nines finger trick

Hold both your hands up and imagine the fingers are numbered 1 to 10 from left to right. Fold down the finger number you want to multiply by 9, then count how many fingers there are to the left to give you the 10s and to the right for the units. For instance, fold down finger number 4 and you will see three fingers to the left to give you 30 and six fingers to the right to give you 6: 4 X 9 = 36.

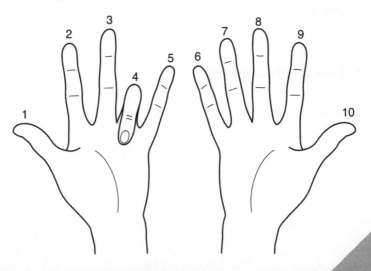

PARENTS' TIP

Sometimes the old methods are still the best. Chanting tables can work for some children, especially if you can make it fun. Choose a time when they wouldn't rather be doing something else – try building it into your walk to school or when you are driving. Recite the tables together and make it a game; test each other and sometimes let your child catch you out. Begin with the easiest, choosing just one a day and work up to occasional, random quick-fire sessions.

Jargon busting

'Multiplication bonds' is another term for times tables, sometimes used by educationalists.

Multiplication

When I was at school, as soon as children had mastered their times tables they moved on to long multiplication sums. This still happens eventually but there are now various steps along the way. This is to ensure that children really understand the concept of multiplication and – in theory – are then less likely to make mistakes.

Arrays

This is likely to be one of the first methods your child will be taught and it uses an array of dots. Children can simply count the dots but the dots can also be partitioned to make calculations simpler.

2 X 15 could be shown:

●●●●●●●●●●●●●●●
●●●●●●●●●●●●●●●

Or partitioned to effectively give two easier sums: 2 X 10 plus 2 X 5:

●●●●●●●●●● ●●●●●
●●●●●●●●●● ●●●●●

Boxes

The next stage is usually to draw boxes with the answer to each part written inside the box. This is to encourage a mental calculation instead of counting dots.

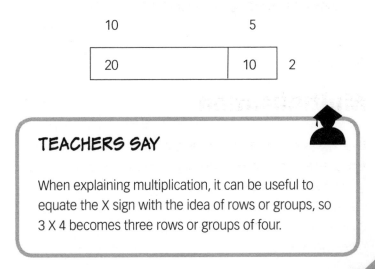

	10	5
	20	10	2

TEACHERS SAY

When explaining multiplication, it can be useful to equate the X sign with the idea of rows or groups, so 3 X 4 becomes three rows or groups of four.

Grid method

Bigger numbers can be handled in the same way by dividing the box into a grid to represent the 10s and units. Again, the answers to each smaller sum are written inside and each individual answer added to give the final total.

47 X 32 would become:

	10	10	10	10	7
10	100	100	100	100	70
10	100	100	100	100	70
10	100	100	100	100	70
2	20	20	20	20	14

Adding each 100, 70, 20 and 14 gives the final answer: 1,504.

PARENTS' TIPS

- When multiplying negatives, remember that when you multiply a positive by a negative the answer is always minus, but a negative times a negative always makes a positive.
- Multiplying doesn't always make numbers bigger. When you times by a fraction the answer is always smaller, for example ½ X 4 = 2.

Division

Chunking is one of the most important of the current methods used in classrooms. It involves grouping chunks of the number being divided and repeated subtraction to achieve the answer. It is probably most easily explained through an example:

```
    35  remainder 3
  7)248
  -  70                    7 X 10 =  70
    178
  - 140                    7 X 20 = 140
     38
  -  35                    7 X  5 =  35
      3
```

In this sum, chunks, or multiples, of 7 are taken away.

PARENTS' TIP

As well as the idea of division being repeated subtraction, it can also help to think of it as sharing – particularly if you give children a practical lesson using a bag of sweets to divide equally with their friends.

Dividing doesn't always make numbers smaller. When you divide by a fraction, the answer will be larger. For example: $8 \div \frac{1}{4} = 32$. Imagine a baker dividing eight cakes into quarters to sell them. How many quarters will the baker have?

Decimals

Multiplying decimals

The simplest solution is to drop the decimal and treat the sum as a long multiplication, and then count the decimal points back in at the end.

2.3 X 3.8 becomes 23 X 38 = 874 and then count in two decimal points to give 8.74

Or if the sum is 2.3 X 0.38 count in three decimal points to give 0.874

It is useful practice to check answers on your calculator.

Dividing decimals

When dividing decimals remember there is no remainder, you add noughts instead.

For example:

2.1 ÷ 5

$$\frac{0.42}{5)2.10}$$

When dividing by a number with a decimal point, rearrange the sum to make the dividing number or divisor a whole number:

1. Draw the dividing box.
2. Ask yourself which number is the dividing number or divisor.
3. Change the divisor to a whole number, multiplying it by 10, 100 or 1,000 as needed.

4. Adjust the number you are dividing in the same way.

For example: 71.13 ÷ 0.2 becomes 711.3 ÷ 2.0

Try 7.5 ÷ 0.02 and 6 ÷ 0.003, checking answers against a calculator.

Multiplying and dividing by 10, 100 and 1,000

It is a useful skill for your child to know instantly what happens when you multiply or divide by 10s, 100s and 1,000s. Practise this by moving the decimal point in each of these:

21.71 X 10	81.14 ÷ 100
54.82 ÷ 10	1.2 X 100
79.63 X 100	5.1 ÷ 100

TEACHERS SAY

Sometimes it pays to wait. Some maths problems occur because the child is not developmentally ready to understand the next stage.

Fractions

Top heavy fractions

Top heavy fractions are where the numerator at the top is larger than the denominator at the bottom; they are also called vulgar or improper fractions.

Mixed numbers

Children are often asked to convert top heavy fractions into mixed numbers.

For example: $\frac{10}{3}$ is the same as $3\frac{1}{3}$

Alternatively, they may be asked to turn a mixed number into a top heavy fraction.

Multiplying fractions

Treat the tops and bottoms separately. Multiply the two numerators together and the two denominators together:

$$\frac{1}{7} \times \frac{2}{3} = \frac{2}{21}$$

Remember you can simplify a fraction diagonally across the times sign:

$\frac{4}{7} \times \frac{14}{16}$ becomes $\frac{1}{1} \times \frac{2}{4} = \frac{2}{4} = \frac{1}{2}$ dividing 4 by 4 and

16 by 4, then 7 by 7 and 14 by 7, simplifying the final answer.

TEACHERS SAY

When multiplying mixed numbers, you cannot multiply the whole numbers first. You must make them into top heavy fractions.

For example: $1\frac{1}{3} \times 2\frac{1}{4} = \frac{4}{3} \times \frac{9}{4} = \frac{1}{1} \times \frac{3}{1} = 3$

Dividing fractions

Just like multiplying except that you turn the second fraction upside down and change the division sign for a multiplication sign.

Remember this little rhyme:

The number you're dividing by
Turn upside down and multiply.

$\frac{2}{5} \div \frac{1}{4}$ becomes $\frac{2}{5} \times \frac{4}{1}$

With mixed numbers the rule is also the same. First turn into top heavy fractions, then change the sign and turn the second fraction upside down.

For example:

$2\frac{1}{2} \div 1\frac{1}{4}$ becomes $\frac{5}{2} \div \frac{5}{4}$ and then $\frac{5}{2} \times \frac{4}{5} = \frac{1}{1} \times \frac{2}{1} = 2$

Percentages

1. The standard school method is to turn the words 20% of 140 into the sum

$$\frac{20}{100} \times \frac{140}{1}$$

and then simplify as for the multiplication of fractions.

2. But there are shortcuts. For most people, working out 50%, or half, of a number is instinctive. 10% is also easy to work out:

$10\% = \frac{10}{100} = \frac{1}{10}$ is the same as divide by 10 or move the decimal point one place to make the number smaller.

For example:

The price is £2.80 but 10% off = £2.80 ÷ 10 = 28 pence.

Once you know what 10% is, you can easily find that 20% is just two lots of 10%; 30% = 10% X 3; 60% = 10% X 6; and so on.

For 5% just halve 10% and for $2\frac{1}{2}\%$, halve 5%.

3. For 1% to 9%, first calculate 1%:

$1\% = \frac{1}{100}$ is the same as divide by 100 or move the decimal point two places.

When you know what 1% is, multiply by 2, 3, 4 and so on to find the percentage you need.

4. To work out something like 65%, break it down to find 50%, 10% and 5%.

TEACHERS SAY

Try to play on your child's strengths when approaching percentages and avoid complicated methods.

Ratios

Use pictures to represent ratios. If there are three girls to every two boys in a class of thirty, keep drawing and repeating the same pattern of three to two to find out how many girls and boys there are in the whole class. Using coloured dots is a clear, easy way to show your answer.

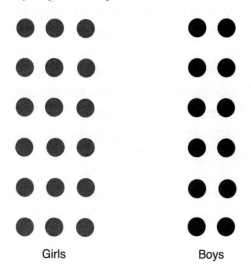

Girls   Boys

Shapes

This is the area of maths that parents will remember as geometry and it is easy to work into everyday life as interesting shapes are everywhere.

There are certain shapes that children will be expected to recognize:

Triangles – three-sided shapes in which the angles add up to 180°. **Equilateral** triangles have three equal sides and three equal angles. **Isosceles triangles** have two equal sides and two equal angles. **Right-angle triangles** have one angle of 90°. **Scalene** triangles have three different length sides (see page 22).

Quadrilaterals – four-sided shapes including.
Square – 1. four equal sides and four right angles.
Rectangle – 2. opposite sides are equal in length and four right angles.
Parallelogram – 3. opposite sides are parallel and equal in length.
Kite – 4. sides vary in length but opposite angles are equal.
Rhombus – 5. four equal sides and opposite angles are equal.
Trapezium – 6. one pair of parallel sides but of different lengths.

Pentagons – these are five-sided shapes and not always so easy to find. Cutting an unripe, unpeeled banana horizontally will often reveal a slightly curved irregular pentagon.

Hexagons – six-sided shapes. Honeycomb is made up of regular hexagons and you can also often find them on footballs.

Heptagons – are seven-sided shapes. The 50 pence and 20 pence coins are both examples of rounded heptagons.

Octagons – have eight sides. Old tiles and churches are good places to look for octagons.

Far less common are ten-sided shapes, or **Decagons,** and **Dodecagons** which have twelve sides.

3-D shapes
Cube – 1. where everything is square like a dice.
Cuboid – 2. a rectangular cube, shaped like a shoe box.
Pyramid – 3. this can be either square or triangular based.
Cylinder – 4. rounded like a biscuit tin.

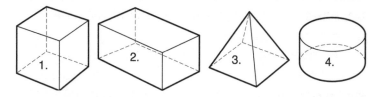

Tessellation
Tessellation – which looks at the way shapes fit exactly together – is an area where art and maths coincide, and it provides lots of practical fun opportunities. Look at intricate

examples in the paintings of M.C. Escher, for instance, or in tile and mosaic patterns. Bees' honeycombs are wonderful naturally-occurring tessellations.

Children enjoy creating their own patterns and interesting – almost 3-D – effects with shapes. Most shapes will fit together nicely although regular pentagons do not, leaving an awkward space in between them.

PARENTS' TIP

Try playing a game of Shape I Spy with your children. You will soon find out that certain shapes are very common but others take some spotting.

Area and perimeter

To avoid any confusion between these two, it's useful to associate measuring the perimeter with a piece of string. At home you can help your child measure the perimeter of all sorts of different objects to see which is the longest.

At school, children usually begin measuring the area of rectangles and triangles by drawing the shape on squared paper and counting up the numbers of squares and half squares.

Rotational symmetry

This refers to the number of times a shape can fit into itself as it is turned through 360º. As an example, a square has rotational symmetry order 4 and a rectangle has rotational symmetry order 2 – this is basically the number of positions in which a shape will look exactly the same when it is turned.

Angles

Practise measuring angles by playing the angle game.

Ask your child to draw five different angles, a mixture of acute, reflex and obtuse. Then make a table:

You both guess what each angle measures before measuring

Angle	Child's guess	Your guess	Angle measurement	Child's score	Your score
1	45°	40°	42°	3	2
2					
3					
4					
5					

with a protractor. The score is how many degrees out you are and the winner is the one with the lowest score. You can play with as many players and angles as you like.

Angle play

Try drawing a triangle of any size. Cut it out and then tear it into three, keeping each angle intact. Since the angles in a triangle always add up to 180º, you will find that the angles will always fit together on a straight line.

Measuring

Many children struggle with measuring even straight lines correctly. This is often simply because they don't position the start of the ruler accurately or don't measure in the right place.

Encourage children by letting them help you when you measure for new household items, such as curtains or a carpet. You can also check the height of doors or appliances. Height charts are another excellent opportunity for measuring and comparing heights, growth rates, as well as different scales of measurement. You can also talk about the importance of choosing the appropriate measure to evaluate different things.

Data Handling

As computers and technology can transform data so efficiently into charts and graphs, there is now generally more emphasis on gathering information and data projects in schools.

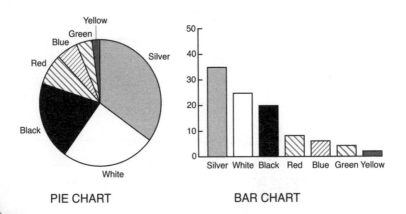

PIE CHART   BAR CHART

You can help your child by setting up your own informal projects at home. For instance, take a survey of the different coloured cars driving past. Look at the best ways of displaying information. Would pie charts or bar graphs work most effectively, or is there something better?

Another simple task is to look at the lengths of words or the numbers of words in a line in a book. Or, try comparing average word lengths in different newspapers.

Five key things you can do to help with maths

1. Practise the times tables. Make it as fun as you can but make sure your child knows them well.

2. Learn the square numbers up to 100. These are almost as useful as the times tables.

3. Make maths and number play part of everyday life. The more familiar your child is, the more confident he or she will be.

4. Never admit to not liking maths yourself.

5. Have fun with numbers – they are just as necessary as words.

THREE
LITERACY

'To acquire the habit of reading is to construct for yourself a refuge from almost all the miseries of life.'
W. SOMERSET MAUGHAM

Make Reading Fun

Alongside fear of maths homework, the other area most likely to cause parents to despair is reading, or more particularly the problem of how to encourage a child to enjoy reading and like books.

If you want your child to be able to write fluently, widen their vocabulary and improve their ability in every other subject, they need to be able to read confidently and with understanding. Ask any primary school teacher what is the single most useful thing you can encourage your child to do and they will all answer 'read more'.

TEACHERS SAY

Children from homes where parents are seen to read, and where books are available and easily accessible, are more likely to become avid readers.

Reading together

- Read to your child everyday and make it part of your daily routine.
- Find, or set out, somewhere comfortable to read.
- Make books fun. Act out the stories, use different voices, be enthusiastic!
- Encourage younger children to make sound effects to accompany the story.
- When children are old enough to read to you, take turns reading and choosing books to share.
- Read chapter books to older children to entice them to read on.
- Talk about the book – look at the language and the way it's set out.
- Even young children can describe the pictures and explain what is going on.
- Ask children what they think will happen next. Build anticipation for tomorrow's instalment.
- Discuss the characters, who they like and why? Or maybe there is someone they dislike?
- Story time can also be a useful opportunity for children to open up about any issues or worries they may have.

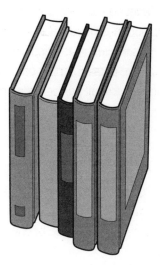

Choosing books

- Make the idea of choosing or buying books a treat.
- Give books as presents for birthdays and for holidays.
- Plan a special outing to a bookshop or library.
- Go along to free story-time sessions at your local library.
- Watch out for author visits to bookshops.
- Spend time with your child talking about titles they might pick.
- Think about the types of stories or non-fiction topics that might interest your child.
- If you are not confident, go along in advance to look at book options.
- Talk to the shop assistant or librarian if you need help choosing books.
- Ask your child's teacher for suggestions for good titles.
- Chat to other parents to find out what books their children enjoy.
- If your child has a short attention span, look at interactive books where they can be involved in the story, or books that have puzzles to solve and activities to complete.
- Remember that not all children learn at the same rate. The important thing is that they enjoy what they read, even if their choice seems too young or simple to you.

PARENTS' TIPS

Some children's reading ability lags behind their vocabulary and comprehension. You may find that this leads to frustration and boredom with the books children can read alone. Story audiobooks are an excellent way of keeping children's interest in stories until they catch up with themselves.

DON'T:

- Dismiss comics and comic books. They can be a fun starting point, particularly if your child relates to pictures and action. For generations, reading the *Beano* has been the first step towards literacy.

DO:

- Stay on the side of encouragement; avoid nagging.
- Look out for book series to encourage continued reading, or other titles by favoured authors.
- Make use of film or TV tie-ins. If a child enjoys the programme, this could be a good way in to books.
- make use of high interest, low vocabulary books to keep the attention of reluctant readers.
- Remember, computers and new technology – electronic books (e-books) and online book groups – may appeal to some children.
- Be seen reading and enjoying books yourself.

Reading Schemes and Teaching Methods

Schools vary in the reading schemes and approaches they take. Most are keen to involve parents and explain their methods. At the very least, your child will probably bring home various reading books and a reading record to which parents are usually asked to contribute.

Phonics

Phonics focus on teaching children to read through the letter sounds. There are two main types of phonics:

- Analytic phonics where children learn whole words first and later break them into their constituent parts, for instance sh-eep.
- Synthetic phonics where children learn the sounds of letters and letter combinations to decode the alphabet, for instance sh-ee-p or c-a-t.

It is only when these sounds are familiar to children that they can progress to reading books. In practice, schools generally teach a combination of both types of phonics and comprehension, working out the meaning of a word from its context or pictures, and through the repetition of specific words.

Research shows that children learn best when school reading schemes are supported by wider reading of 'real' books and other material at home.

Getting the Most From What You Read

Fiction

Help your child learn how to look at language, layout and meaning when they read. From an early age encourage children to describe the pictures in their books and explain

what's happening; in effect encourage them to tell the story. Predicting what might happen next or speculating on a character's motives develop your child's interest and involvement in a story and help their comprehension.

These are all invaluable skills when children come to write their own stories. Don't be afraid to be critical of what you read – talk about what you both like and dislike about a story. Look at the characters. Ask children who they like and dislike, and why they empathize with certain personalities or traits. What motivates the characters? Identify features that an author has used to manipulate their readers' reactions. This will help when children are asked to review books for homework.

Also talk about the way the pictures work with the text. Do they simply show what is happening in the story or do they give you more detail? Ask your child to really imagine a character or scene. Do the illustrations match their imagination? Does it help to have pictures? Perhaps some children may prefer their own mental images.

TEACHERS SAY

Take time to think about the books your child tends to choose, the authors and genres he or she prefers. Are there ways to develop these preferences and set personal challenges? For example, at the beginning of a long school holiday children could perhaps aim to find four books – by new authors or in different genres – to read before the new term starts.

Develop reading skills by scanning a page for:

- Specific letter groups or words.
- Descriptive words or phrases.
- Unusual words for which you can look up the meaning.

Also:

- Look at how language is used to create atmosphere and imagery.
- Discuss any moral dilemmas raised by what you have read.
- Talk about what has happened so far and what you think might happen next. What clues has the author offered and how do they help you understand the story?

Look out for

Allegories – a piece of writing or picture which carries another, deeper meaning or moral truth.

Similes – figures of speech that draw a comparison between two different things, or more often a person to a thing. They usually contain the words 'as' or 'like', for example: 'He had a face like thunder'; 'Run like the wind'; or 'She was as white as a sheet'.

Metaphors – a condensed simile without the words 'as' or 'like'. Metaphors are words or phrases which describe a person or a thing as if they were something that they could not literally be. For example: 'That teacher is a dragon' or 'The river snaked through the valley'.

Synonyms – words with similar meanings, for example: power, strength, control. A thesaurus will suggest lots of examples. Synonyms are useful when an author wants to avoid repetition.

Antonyms – words with opposite meanings, for example: tiny and huge, or strong and weak.

Puns – plays on words that can be either the same word with different meanings or words that sound alike, e.g. 'Without geometry, life is pointless' and 'A backward poet wrote inverse'.

Paradoxes – statements that seem to contradict themselves but contain a truth, e.g. 'More haste, less speed'.

Hyperbole – deliberate exaggeration for effect or to create an impression. For example: 'We waited in the queue for days' and 'I could eat a horse'.

Oxymoron – a phrase containing words or ideas that contradict each other, e.g. 'a silent cheer' or 'an open secret'.

Clichés – phrases or expressions that began as useful metaphors but have been so overused that they have become predictable or boring. Good examples are: 'Actions speak louder than words', or even 'Once upon a time …'

Tautology – the repetition of different words with the same meaning – and best avoided. 'Very unique', 'added extra', 'close proximity' and 'the reason is because' are some examples. See how many you can spot on news reports, in advertising and normal conversation.

Poetry

Many of the first books we share with small children are written in rhyme. The rhythm and sound of the words appeal to children and remain in their memories. As they grow older, they continue to enjoy different types of poetry and songs. Reading poems can increase children's vocabulary, and word play that uses rhyme also boosts fluency.

When reading a poem, ask what type of poem it is:

- Does it rhyme?
- Is it a narrative poem telling a story?
- A nonsense poem?
- A haiku? (see below)
- A shape poem? (see opposite)

Haikus – A haiku is a traditional Japanese form of poetry that has become very popular. It consists of three lines that rarely rhyme. The first and last lines have five syllables each, and the middle line has seven.

Traditionally, haikus use ordinary language and are often about animals or the natural world. They can be used to record a specific incident or to describe something.

Shape poems – These are poems in which the arrangement of the words is as important as the words themselves in expressing meaning. They are sometimes called visual or pattern poems. They can rhyme – although this is not essential – and they are an ancient form of poetry. The earliest known example dates from 300 BC and was written by the Greek poet Simias of Rhodes. It is in the shape of an axe to represent the axe used to build the Trojan Horse through which the ancient Greeks entered and invaded Troy.

Look out for

Alliteration – the repetition of sounds (usually consonants) at the beginnings of words to create an atmosphere or a feeling. Alliteration is also commonly used in tongue twisters such as, 'She sells seashells on the seashore', and advertising slogans like, 'You'll never put a better bit of butter on your knife'.

Assonance – similar to alliteration but repeats vowel sounds with different consonants, or the same consonants with different vowels, in order to create effect, e.g. 'On a proud round cloud in a white high night' or 'Season of mists and mellow fruitfulness'.

Imagery – creating vivid mental pictures or sensations by comparing one thing to another. Similes and metaphors help create imagery.

Personification – a type of metaphor where human characteristics are attached to an animal or thing, as in 'The wind spoke of far flung shores'.

Onomatopoeia – words which suggest what they are describing through their sound. Good examples are 'swish', 'buzz', 'mumble' and 'miaow'.

Non-fiction

You may find that your child prefers reading non-fiction books on a topic that interests him or her. Again, choosing something that appeals and holds attention is vital.

Non-fiction books are also important to use as reference for homework and project work. Learning how to find relevant information quickly is a useful skill.

- Scan for information – practise skimming a page to pick out key words or phrases.
- Check chapter titles and page headings to direct your search.
- Study the pictures and read any captions.
- Learn to spot names and dates.
- As children get older, encourage them to make short notes as they read; this will fix facts in their minds and it is a useful habit to have when homework becomes more complex.
- Use notes to gather evidence to explain events or support ideas.
- Newspapers, and in particular the weekend papers, often have sections for young readers with some news stories and information but also puzzles, crosswords and other activities.
- Try looking at the ways different newspapers tell the same story and note how opposite viewpoints are expressed.

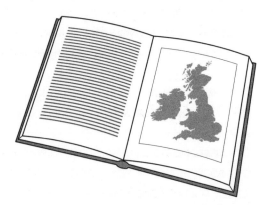

TEACHERS SAY

To help comprehension, look at adverts in magazines and newspapers with your child. Look at the words and phrases they use. What are they not telling you? Ask what the advert is trying to do.

Dictionaries

- Make a habit of looking up the meaning of unfamiliar words in the dictionary. This can be more fun for younger children if you use a picture dictionary.
- Specialist dictionaries are also available; these are packed with information on wildlife, science or history, for example.
- Play games like Scrabble with a dictionary on hand to help find words.
- Looking up words in a dictionary helps children to automatically sort letters and words into alphabetical order.
- Take it in turns to find an unusual word in the dictionary. Everyone else then tries to guess the meaning. See who can come up with the most difficult word. This works well if it becomes part of your daily routine, with one new word a day.

TEACHERS SAY

Use a thesaurus to look up synonyms and antonyms to help make written work more interesting. Online dictionaries and thesauruses are useful tools for children.

Writing

Writing ability develops alongside reading. Learning how to structure their work, spelling, grammar and punctuation skills help children share ideas, tell a story, write a letter or even a piece of non-fiction.

Spelling

Learning a list of spellings is really no different from memorizing anything else.

- Read through the new words slowly and carefully a few times.
- Next, try writing the words from memory.
- Check your list against the original one.
- Rewrite correctly any words that are wrong.
- Go back to the list after an hour and recheck.
- If everything is correct, recheck the next day.

Regularly returning to the list after some time away will help to fix words in your child's mind.

Helpful rules

Over 10 per cent of English words are not spelt in the way they sound. Luckily, there are rules you can learn to help. Unfortunately, you also need to know the exceptions.

I before E

I before E, except after C
Or when sounded like A
As in neigh, weigh and sleigh.

Remember: Receive a Piece of Pie.

There is also:

I before E, except after C
Though Weird is just Weird.

And so are neighbour, height, foreign, heir and forfeit, to name but a few. So a better version could be:

I before E, except after C but only if the sound is 'ee'.
For everything else it tends to be 'ei'.

A notable exception is the word 'friend' which can be remembered by:

You always need friends to the end.

And there are also protein, seize, weir, counterfeit and caffeine, among others.

Other major exceptions are

- Words where the 'c' is pronounced 'sh', when I comes before E after the letter C, for example: species, ancient and efficient.
- Plurals of words ending in 'cy' which become 'cies', for example: delicacy/delicacies, fancy/fancies and policy/policies.

Is it '-eed' or '-ede'?

- If the word begins with 'ex-', 'pro-' or 'suc-', then use '-eed', e.g. exceed, proceed, succeed (note the double 'cc').
- For everything else, it is usually '-ede', e.g. concede, intercede, precede.

Plurals

The general rule is to add an 's' as in the word plural/plurals. As always in the English language, this does not apply at all times.

- Add 'es' to words which end in the letters 's', 'x', 'z', 'ch' or 'sh': pass/passes, fox/ foxes, buzz/buzzes, church/churches, push/pushes.
- If a word ends in a consonant followed by a 'y', lose the 'y' and add 'ies': fairy/fairies, party/parties, bully/bullies.
- Where a word ends with a vowel followed by a 'y', keep the 'y' and add an 's': day/days, delay/delays, monkey/monkeys.

For words ending in 'o' add an 's' or 'es':

- Where there is a vowel followed by the 'o' just add 's': studio/studios, stereo/stereos, piano/pianos.
- There are probably more words ending in 'o' where you just add the 's' but there are exceptions, such as: echoes, heroes, mosquitoes, potatoes, tomatoes.

- Some words ending in 'o' can be spelt both with an 's' and 'es': avocados/avocadoes, ghettos/ghettoes, mementos/mementoes.
- There are words which take the same form whether singular or plural, for example: species, sheep, fish, aircraft.
- There are also words which change when they become plural, for example: child/children, goose/geese, mouse/mice.

Words ending in 'f' or 'fe' are not always consistent:
- Most drop the 'f' and add '-ves' for the plural, for example: calf/calves, wife/wives, knife/knives, thief/thieves and loaf/loaves.
- However there are exceptions: roofs, beliefs, chiefs.
- And some words can be either: hoofs/hooves, wharfs/wharves.
- If a word ends in double 'f', just add 's': cliff/cliffs.

Adding prefixes
Common prefixes are 'mis-', dis-', 'un-' and 'in-'. Do not add or take away any letters – mis-understood, mis-spell, dis-appear, dis-satisfied, un-successful, un-necessary, in-secure, in-excusable.

TEACHERS SAY

Children will need to listen very carefully to hear the difference in stress and sound when they pronounce words.

Adding suffixes

Suffixes are added at the end of a word and the rules are slightly more complex.

Double the final consonant:

- When a word ends in a consonant following a vowel, e.g. flat/flatter.
- When the suffix begins with a vowel, e.g. '-er', '-ed', '-able' and '-ing'.
- The word has only a single short vowel, e.g. hop/hopping.
- Where words end in 'l' following a single vowel, e.g. travel/travelling.
- In longer words where the stress is on the second syllable or vowel when you say them aloud, e.g. begin/beginning, admit/admitted.

Do not double the final consonant in longer words where the stress falls on the first syllable or vowel, e.g. enter/entered, happen/happening.

Words ending in silent 'e':

- Usually keep the final 'e' before an ending that begins with a consonant, e.g. hopeful, completely.
- Usually drop the 'e' before suffixes that begin with a vowel, e.g. hoping, completing.
- There are exceptions to keep the vowel sound long, e.g. saleable, which keep the final 'e'.
- The 'e' also remains to maintain the pronunciation of words with a soft 'c' or 'g', e.g. noticeable, manageable, peaceable.
- Words ending in 'oe' always keep the 'e', e.g. canoeing.

Words ending in 'y':

- If the letter before the 'y' is a consonant, then change the 'y' to 'i', e.g. envy, envied.
- But keep the 'y' if the suffix is '-ing', e.g. cry, cries, cried, crying.
- Also keep the 'y' where the letter before the 'y' is a vowel, e.g. annoy, annoyance.

Words ending with 'ac' or 'ic':

- Add a 'k' before the ending, e.g. traffic/trafficking, picnic/picnicked.

Double 'll':

- Words ending with 'll' drop one 'l' when they are joined in compound words, e.g. all + though = although, full+ fill = fulfil.

Homophones

These are words that sound alike but which are spelt differently and have completely different meanings. Here are some common examples:

Aloud and allowed   *Bare and bear*
Beach and beech   *Boy and buoy*
Fair and fare   *Hair and hare*
Here and hear
Know and no
Pair and pear
Plain and plane
Read and reed
Red and read
See and sea   *There and their*

Too and two
Where and wear
Would and wood

Weather and whether
Which and witch
Write and right

TEACHERS SAY

The more children read, the better their spelling, grammar and punctuation will become. The most interesting written work comes from children who read widely.

Homographs

Homographs are words which have different meanings but are spelt the same, although sometimes they are pronounced differently, e.g. bass = a sea fish, and bass = a deep voice.

Practice or practise?

The answer, of course, is both but how do you know which one to choose?

- Practice with a 'c' is the noun, e.g. 'I have finished my piano practice'.
- Practise with an 's' is the verb, e.g. 'I practised the piano'.

Even so, it is not always easy to work out which is the correct choice in a sentence.

PARENTS' TIP

Try swapping practice or practise for advice (the noun) or advise (the verb). The different sounds should make it easier to decide which to use:
'I adviced for an hour' should clearly be 'I advised for an hour', and in the same way, 'I practised for an hour'.

Affecting effects

Affect is the verb and effect is the noun. Use the word raven to remember the difference:

R emember
A ffect
V erb
E ffect
N oun

Stationary stationer

To be clear on the difference between stationary and stationery:

A station stands still – it is stationary.

A stationer sells stationery.

And: pens are stationery, while parked cars are stationary.

Desert desserts

A desert is sandy with only one 's'.

While desserts have two 'ss' for sweet stuff, strawberry shortcake and two helpings of pudding.

Mnemonics to help you remember

Some spellings seem to defy all rules and the only answer is to learn them individually. There are some age-old mnemonic phrases you probably remember from your own schooldays, which are still useful for children today and are fun to know.

Argument
Argue lost an 'e' in argument.

Arithmetic
A Rat In The House Might Eat The Ice Cream.

Ascertain
When you ascertain a fact, always be As Certain as you possibly can.

Beautiful
Big Elephants Are Usually BEAUtiful.

Because
Big Elephants Can Always Understand Small Elephants.

Chaos

Cyclones, Hurricanes And Other Storms
create chaos.

Committee

Many Meetings Take Time – Everyone's Exhausted.

Difficulty

Mrs D, Mrs I, Mrs FFI, Mrs C, Mrs U, Mrs LTY.

Diarrhoea

Dash In A Real Rush. Hurry Or Else Accident.

Doubt

It's only natural to Be in doubt.

Eczema

Even Clean ZEbras MAy get eczema.

Geography

General Eisenhower's Old Grandfather Rode A Pig Home
Yesterday.

Hear, here

You hear with your ear.

Innocent

IN NO CENTury is murder an innocent crime.

Mnemonics
Mnemonics Now Erase Man's Oldest Nemesis: Insufficient Cerebral Storage.

Necessary
Never Eat Crisps, Eat Salad Sandwiches And Remain Young.

Necessary for Success
Only one 'C' is necessary but you need two 'Cs' for success.

Mississippi
Mrs M, Mrs I, Mrs SSI, Mrs SSI, Mrs PPI.

Ocean
Only Cats' Eyes Are Narrow.

People
People Eat Other People's Leftovers Eagerly.

Potassium
One tea and two sugars.

Principled principals
Your princiPAL is your PAL, while the ruLES he enforces are called principLES.

Rhythm
Rhythm Has Your Two Hips Moving.

Separate

Sep A Rat E!

Slaughter

Slaughter is simply laughter with an 'S' at the start.

Subtle

Be subtle, be silent.

There or Their?

There is either HERE or THERE and HERE can be found in THERE.

A person is an HEIR before they inherit THEIR fortune.

Together

If you go To Get Her, you'll be together.

Wednesday

We Do Not Eat Soup Day.

Woolly

W, double 'o', double 'l', y.

You can use the same idea for coolly.

PARENTS' TIP

Children love making up their own mnemonics; the sillier the idea the easier it will be to remember!

Grammar

The various types of words in sentences all have different names known as the 'parts of speech'. There is an old poem, once commonly taught in classrooms, which helps to remind you what each does:

The parts of speech

Every name is called a Noun
Like field and fountain, street and town.

In place of a noun the Pronoun stands
For he, she and it can clap their hands.

An Adjective describes a thing
Like magic wand and feathered wing.

The Verb means action, something done
To read, to write, to walk, to run.

How things are done, the Adverbs tell
Like quickly, slowly, badly, well.

A Preposition shows relation
Like in the street, or at the station.

Conjunctions join in different ways
Sentences, words, or thought and phrase.

The Interjection suggests surprise
As Oh! How splendid! Oh my! You're wise!

Through poetry we learn how each
Of these make up the parts of speech.

Nouns and verbs

When we speak, most of us automatically form logical sentences without thinking about what goes into creating them. It is worth analysing the components of fluent, written English.

To form a simple sentence you always need at least one noun and one verb. The noun is the subject of the sentence, the thing or person doing or being something. The verb is the action or activity. Many sentences also contain a direct object, a second noun, which is the person or thing affected by the action.

For example, in the simple sentence 'Tom threw the ball', 'Tom' is the subject, 'threw' is the verb and 'the ball' is the direct object.

Common nouns – Common nouns are the general names of people, places and things. If you can put the words 'a', 'an', or 'the' in front of a word, then it is probably a common noun. Teenager, island, computer and dog are all everyday examples. As these are general names, they do not need capital letters unless they are at the beginning of a sentence or part of a title.

Proper nouns – Proper nouns name specific people, places and things, and so always begin with a capital letter. Here are some examples to show the difference:

Common noun	Proper noun
teenager	Ted
girl	Elizabeth
country	France
island	Bermuda
computer	MacBook
coffee shop	Starbucks
dog	Lassie
month	May
town	Ashford
city	Rome

Capital letters are also used for dates or special holidays, specific events in history such as battles, and religious names.

Abstract nouns – These are nouns which are ideas, feelings or experiences. They do not physically exist as an object and they cannot be detected with any of the five senses. Kindness, excitement, love, anger and friendship are all examples.

Did you know?
'A' and 'an' are known as the indefinite articles as they are introducing a noun that is not a specific object. 'The' is known as the definite article as it is talking about a specific object or person.

Collective nouns – Collective nouns for groups of people or things take a singular verb when viewed as a single, complete unit, e.g. 'The class is small'. But when the class is viewed as a number of separate individuals a plural verb is used, e.g. 'The class were arguing'.

Other collective nouns include: family, group, bunch, team, choir, collection, audience, army, parliament and jury.

There are also many examples of collective nouns for animals. Your children are probably familiar with some of the more common ones such as a flock of sheep or birds, a herd of cows and a pride of lions, but do you remember some of the stranger examples which date back centuries?

A sleuth of bears.   A wake of buzzards.
A float of crocodiles.   A murder of crows.
A charm of finches.   A skein of goslings.
A scold of jays.   An exultation of larks.

A labour of moles.   A troop of monkeys.

A yoke of oxen.   An ostentation of peacocks.

A storytelling of ravens.   A parliament of rooks.

A murmuration of starlings.   A bale of turtles.

An eyrar or bevy of swans.

A pod of pelicans, dolphins or whales.

Pronouns

Pronouns take the place of nouns. They help to make sentences more interesting and avoid repetition. Words like 'she', 'his', 'it', 'that' and 'I' are all pronouns. Unless they start a sentence, they are not usually capitalized (with the exception of I).

Personal pronouns – Personal pronouns stand in for people or things.

'I', 'you', 'he', 'she', 'we', 'they', 'them', 'us', 'me', 'her' and 'him' are all personal pronouns for people or animals.

'It', 'they' and 'them' are personal pronouns for things.

Personal pronouns can also be the subject of the sentence (for example, 'I', 'you', 'he' and 'we') or the object, the who or what that is being affected by the action (for instance, 'me' and 'it'). Some personal pronouns are the same, whether the subject or the object in a sentence. There are also possessive pronouns to show that something belongs to someone and reflexive pronouns that refer back to a person or thing that has already been mentioned.

Subject	Object	Possessive	Reflexive
I	me	mine	myself
you	you	yours	yourself
you (plural)	you	yours	yourselves
she	her	hers	herself
he	him	his	himself
it	it	its	itself
they	them	theirs	themselves
we	us	ours	ourselves

Relative pronouns – 'That', 'this', 'which', 'who', 'whom', 'whose', 'where', 'when', 'why', 'whoever' and 'whichever' are all common examples of relative pronouns. These are words that link two clauses in a sentence and relate them to each other. 'This is the house that Jack built' is a well-known example.

TEACHERS SAY

Pronouns are vital in making a piece of writing flow. Nevertheless, it's important to read through the text carefully, to make sure their use has not made the meaning unclear.

Common confusions
I and me

Children, as well as some adults, struggle to work out when to use 'I' and when to use 'me' correctly in a sentence. In fact, the problem only arises when you (as I or me) are not alone.

You would never write 'Me went to the cinema', but you might write 'Jo and me went to the cinema', instead of the correct 'Jo and I went to the cinema'.

Always try to remember whether you would use 'I' or 'me' in a sentence if there was not an extra person. Look at these two sentences:

The man handed Jo and me our tickets.

Or:

The man handed Jo and I our tickets.

If you remove Jo, it is obvious that the first version is right as you would never say 'The man handed I a ticket'.

To use the correct grammatical terms, 'I' is used when you are the subject noun, the person doing the action. 'Me' is used as the object noun, when you are the person affected by the action or verb.

More about verbs

To explain when something is taking place – in the past, present or future – the tense of the verb must change. We often only think about verb tenses when we are learning a foreign language but knowing when to use each form is just as important in English.

The two most frequently used verbs are 'to be' and 'to have'. These are very useful on their own but they are also key in the formation of different tenses.

To be

Present tense	Past tense
I am	I was
You are	You were
He/she/it is	He/she/it was
We are	We were
You are (plural)	You were
They are	They were

To have

Present tense	Past tense
I have	I had
You have	You had
He/she/it has	He/she/it had
We have	We had
You have (plural)	You had
They have	They had

Present tense – At its simplest, the present tense uses the verb without the infinitive 'to' at the beginning. It is used for things you do regularly and for facts, for example: 'I walk' and 'He acts'.

The **present continuous tense** is used for something that is happening now, and adds 'to be' as an auxiliary verb, for example: 'I am walking' and 'He is acting'.

Past tense – The past tense changes the verb to show that an action happened in the past. For example: 'I walked' and 'He acted'.

This is often done simply by adding '-ed' to the ed of the verb, although there are many exceptions or irregular verbs.

Past continuous or imperfect tense – This tense adds the past tense of 'to be' as an auxiliary verb to show that an action took place over a long period of time. For example: 'I was walking' and 'He was acting'.

Future tense – Strictly speaking there is no distinct future tense in English, although there are of course ways to show that something will happen in the future.

One of the most obvious is to use verbs such as 'will', 'shall' or 'going to' as auxiliary verbs to the action. For example: 'I will walk later' and 'He is going to act'.

TEACHERS SAY

A common mistake is to use the preposition 'of' in place of an auxiliary verb. How many times have you heard, 'I could of done that …' or 'I must of made a mistake'? These are wrong. 'Of' is not a verb.

These sentences should be: 'I could have done that' and 'I must have made a mistake'.

Auxiliary verbs – Auxiliary or helping verbs are used with the main verb to alter its meaning. Examples include: do, does, did, will, would, could, can, shall, should, may, might, must, ought.

Common confusions
If I was or If I were?

It is almost never correct to say 'I were' rather than 'I was', but there are times when it is correct to say, 'If I were …' It all depends on the context. The easiest way to know which to use is to think if something is true or possible, or not.

For instance, 'If I was at home yesterday when Sue called, I didn't hear her knock'. This is something that could be true and is certainly not impossible. The grammatical term for this is indicative.

But in a scenario where something could never be the case, 'If I were you, I'd take a chance'. I could never be you and so this is supposing the impossible and in this instance it is right to use 'I were'. This is an example of the subjunctive tense.

Split infinitives – A split infinitive occurs when another word is placed between the infinitive 'to' and the verb. One of the most famous examples is the 'To boldly go' from the opening sequence of *Star Trek*: To boldly go where no man has gone before.

Traditionally, this used to be considered bad grammar but one of the exciting things about language is the way it evolves and adapts over time. Rules of grammar are now more relaxed and many people feel that it is perfectly acceptable to use split infinitives.

Mixed tenses – Verbs within a sentence should agree with one another, for instance, it is incorrect to say, 'I should be glad if you will meet me'. The sentence should be: 'I should be glad if you would meet me.'

Passed and past – Passed is the action and therefore the verb:

Josh passed Ollie the ball.

For anything else use 'past', which can be a noun, adjective, adverb or preposition:

Noun: 'It happened in the past.'
Adjective: 'In past decades …'
Adverb: 'He drove past the house.'
Preposition: 'Jan walked past me.'

Adjectives

Adjectives provide more information about nouns. They are describing words and add interest to language.

Comparative and superlative – Adjectives can also be used to compare. Comparative adjectives such as 'better' and 'taller' compare two people or things, while superlatives such as 'best' and 'tallest' apply to three or more, comparing something to the rest of its group.

> *Sandra is the shorter of the two sisters.*
But: *Sandra is the shortest of the three girls.*

Examples of one- and two-syllable adjectives:

Adjective	Comparative	Superlative
big	bigger	biggest
wise	wiser	wisest
tall	taller	tallest
rich	richer	richest
narrow	narrower	narrowest
happy	happier	happiest
easy	easier	easiest

Adjectives with more than two syllables, or those which end in '-ous', '-ing', '-ed' and '-ful' (such as beautiful, amazing, excited or scrumptious), add 'more' for the comparative and 'most' for the superlative:

That lesson was more boring than last week's.
She was the most famous actress in the play.

Adjective	Comparative	Superlative
peaceful	more peaceful	most peaceful
thoughtful	more thoughtful	most thoughtful
pleasant	more pleasant	most pleasant
amazing	more amazing	most amazing
generous	more generous	most generous
wicked	more wicked	most wicked
excited	more excited	most excited
beautiful	more beautiful	most beautiful
popular	more popular	most popular
intelligent	more intelligent	most intelligent

Odd ones out:

Adjective	Comparative	Superlative
good	better	best
bad	worse	worst
little	less	least
many/much	more	most
far	further	furthest
fun	more fun	most fun

Adverbs

In the same way that an adjective describes a noun, an adverb provides more detail about the verb. For example, 'I walked briskly'. Again, adverbs help to make a composition or speech more interesting and give extra information. Many adverbs end in '-ly' – just think of lovely, wisely, noisily and quietly – but there are also others – such as quite, fast, almost and never.

Some words can be both adverbs and adjectives, depending on how they are used.

He ran fast.

The word 'fast' is an adverb when it is describing the verb 'ran', but it is an adjective when it describes the athlete:

The athlete was fast.

Adverbs can also be used to give more detail about other adverbs:

The athlete ran incredibly fast.

They can even be applied to adjectives:

The pine tree was extremely tall.

Sentences

Sentences also contain phrases and clauses to make them more interesting or to provide more information.

Phrases – can be nouns, adjectives or adverbs. They are groups of words added to sentences to provide more detail. They do not usually contain a verb and would make little sense without the rest of the sentence. These are examples of different types of phrase:

To run fast requires training.
'To run fast' acts as the noun, the verb is 'requires'.

My friend, wearing a red scarf, is sitting on the step.
'Wearing a red scarf' is an adjective phrase, describing the friend in greater detail.

Liz held her breath for as long as she could.
'For as long as she could' is an adverb phrase, giving more information about the action.

Clauses – are a group of words containing a subject and a verb, and are almost a sentence within a sentence. There may be more than one clause in a sentence and there are two basic types, the main clause and the subordinate clause.

Main clause – this is the most important clause and could be a sentence on its own. There can be two main clauses of equal importance, both of which could work alone. For example:
I threw the ball and the dog chased it.

Subordinate clause – just like a phrase, a subordinate clause can be used as the noun, adjective or adverb, and depends upon the main clause.

• Noun clause:
Where she hid it will never be known.
'Where she hid it' is the subject noun, or noun clause.
> *I do not know where to look first.*

'Where to look first' is the object noun, or noun clause.

• Adjective clause:
I found the key that I had been searching for.
'That I had been searching for' is the adjective clause as it describes the key.

• Adverb clause:
I searched for the key while I talked on my mobile.
'While I talked on my mobile' is the adverb clause as it gives extra detail about the action, in this instance, the search for the key.

Complex and compound sentences – a sentence containing a main clause and one or more subordinate clauses is called a complex sentence. A compound sentence contains more that one main clause joined by 'but', 'or', 'and', for instance: 'I found the key and finished my telephone conversation.' It may also contain subordinate clauses.

Conjunctions

Conjunctions join words, phrases and clauses. There are four types:

Coordinating conjunctions – words such as 'and', 'but', 'or' and 'so' which link parts of a sentence of equal importance. This is a well-known – although slightly odd – acronym to remind you of the coordinating conjunctions:

> BOAF SYN
> **B** ut
> **O** r
> **A** nd
> **F** or
> **S** o
> **Y** et
> **N** or

Subordinate conjunctions – join a less important clause to a more important one. 'Although', 'because', 'since', 'unless', 'as' and 'while' can all be used as subordinating conjunctions. In the following sentence, the fact that she went to the park is more important:

> *She went to the park because it was sunny.*

Compound conjunctions – use more than one word and often include 'as' or 'that'. Common examples include 'as soon as', 'in order that', 'provided that'.

> *I will go for a walk as long as it's not cold.*
> *Liz divided the cake so that everyone could have a piece.*

Correlative conjunctions – compare or relate one thing to another. 'Not only … but also', 'neither … nor', 'whether … or' and 'the more … the less' can all be used.

The more I see of him, the more I like him.
Not only is she my sister, she is also my friend.
Whether we eat out or stay in doesn't make a difference to me.

Common confusions
As and like
You often hear people using the word 'like' in phrases such as 'She thinks like I do'. This is actually incorrect. The word 'like' can be used as an adjective or a preposition but it is not a conjunction. Use the word 'as' if what you are really saying is 'in the same way that'.
She thinks as I do.

Prepositions
Prepositions link nouns, pronouns and phrases to other words in a sentence. For example, in the sentence 'The book is on the desk', 'on' is the preposition. The word or phrase that is introduced by the preposition is called the object of the preposition. It can be hard to know which preposition is correct.

Here are some which are often confused:
- Different *from* or to (not 'than')
- Anxious *about* (not 'of')
- Prefer this *to* that (not 'than')
- Bored *by* or *with* (not 'of')
- Cover with (not 'by')

Punctuation

To a degree, punctuation can be a matter of personal preference. Some people like to use it more than others but there are some basic rules which need to be followed in order to make meaning clear. It is also important to be consistent in style.

Full stop

Perhaps the most important of all punctuation, full stops show where a sentence ends. They mark the point at which you would pause if you were speaking aloud.

- A full stop can also indicate an abbreviation, where a word has been shortened (for example, Feb. for February), although it is becoming increasingly common not to use one.
- It is not usual to use a full stop where an abbreviated word still keeps the final letter, for instance in titles such as Mr, Mrs and Dr (unless they come at the end of a sentence).
- They are unnecessary in acronyms like BBC, TV, MP and USA.
- If a sentence finishes with an abbreviation and full stop, you do not need an extra full stop.

PARENTS' TIP

It often helps children to imagine they are speaking out loud when trying to decide what punctuation to use. When they speak, they change expression and tone; they also pause so that people can understand exactly what they mean. Punctuation does the same job when they are writing.

Other stops

Sentences can also end with a question mark or an exclamation mark.

Question marks

- Use a question mark for all direct questions, for example: 'What time will he arrive?'
- Do not use a question mark for indirect, reported questions, for example: 'I wonder what time he will arrive.'

TEACHERS SAY

Children sometimes have trouble spotting when a sentence really is a question. Challenge each other to change sentences from statements into direct and indirect questions.

Exclamation marks

- Exclamation marks are used for emphasis, for instance, 'Fire! Fire!'
- They can also express emotion, particularly anger, fear, surprise or happiness, for example, 'I don't believe it!'
- Exclamation marks are used to show sound effects. 'Pow!' or 'Whoosh!' are typical examples and often appear in comic strips.
- They are the written equivalent of shouting, so should be used with care.

- People have become very used to using them in text messages and there is a danger of using too many of them in any piece of writing! It can be distracting!!

If a question mark or an exclamation mark follow an abbreviation, it used to be common practice to keep the full stop before the extra mark, e.g. 'Feb.!', although nowadays it is more common for the extra mark to replace the full stop, e.g. 'Feb!'

Capital letters

Capital letters are used to start every new sentence (unless you are ee cummings!) Also use capital letters for:

- All proper nouns and names.
- All adjectives which come from proper nouns, for example, English or Victorian.
- The first and all main words in the titles of books, films, plays, magazines and newspapers.
- The titles of companies and people.
- The start of each new line of traditional poems.

Commas

Commas mark a shorter pause than full stops. They are also used:
- To separate words in a list.
- Between phrases and clauses in a sentence.
- Between a series of adjectives, for example: 'It was a soft, red, woolly scarf.'

TEACHERS SAY

It is easy to change the meaning of a sentence by putting the comma in the wrong place. Play around with your children to see how commas work.
Compare:
Meg likes Anna, who plays tennis a lot more than I do.
And:
Meg likes Anna, who plays tennis, a lot more than I do.

- Also between a series of adverbs: 'He worked quickly, quietly and confidently.'
- When a phrase or clause within a sentence gives extra information: 'Ella's room, which was south-facing, was very sunny.' Brackets or dashes could also be used for this.
- Sometimes, before a name, for example: 'Watch out, Max!'
- Or even either side of a name, for example: 'Her brother, George, is older.'

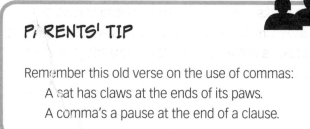

PARENTS' TIP

Remember this old verse on the use of commas:
    A cat has claws at the ends of its paws.
    A comma's a pause at the end of a clause.

Speech marks

Direct speech always needs inverted commas around it but the speech can come at the beginning or end of a sentence, or it can even be interrupted in the middle. However it is set out, any punctuation always comes within the speech marks:

> *Becca said, 'I am going away on holiday.'*
> *'Where are you going?' asked Jess.*
> *'To France,' Becca replied. 'To stay with my aunt.'*

- When the speech comes at the end of the sentence, there should be a comma before the inverted comma.
    > *Becca said, 'I am going on holiday.'*
- When the speech comes first, if it does not form a question, it should end with a comma before the speech mark:
    > *'I leave on Friday,' said Becca.*
- Interrupted speech can also form one sentence:
    > *'I'm going,' said Becca, 'to visit my aunt.'*

Some people favour single and some double inverted commas. Both are fine but it is worth finding out which ones a teacher prefers. Whichever you choose, always stick with the same style throughout a piece of work.

Speech marks or inverted commas can also be called quotation marks –this is a useful way to remind children to always use them when quoting someone's words or a passage from a book, as well as for the title of something like a book, magazine, film or programme.

- When you need speech marks within speech marks (for instance, for a title within a speech), use double inside single, or the other way around:

  'I went to see "Eclipse",' said Astrid.

Or: *"I went to see 'Eclipse'," said Astrid.*

- If you are working on a computer, titles can be put into italic type instead of using inverted commas.

Apostrophes

There are two reasons for using an apostrophe. The first is with a noun to show possession and the second is to signal that letters have been left out in a word.

Possession – Single nouns add apostrophe 's' to show ownership, for instance:

> The cat's hat.
> George's room.

If the noun ends in the letter 's', you still add apostrophe 's':

> Janis's picture.
> The princess's crown.

Plural nouns can vary. Where the plural ends in 's', simply add an apostrophe after the letter:

> The cats' dinner.
> The girls' books.

If the plural does not end in the letter 's' – for example, men, women, children – add an apostrophe and an 's':

> The men's coats.
> The children's game.

Missing letters – Letters are sometimes missed out to make a word – or more often two words – shorter. This is called a contraction and is very common in speech. The apostrophe is placed where the missing letter, which is often an 'o', should be:

do not	don't
are not	aren't
could not	couldn't
were not	weren't

There are a couple of exceptions:

shall not – shan't
will not – won't

Common confusions

- It makes no difference if the thing that is owned is singular or plural, just check whether there is one or more owner.
- Pronouns such as hers, his, yours, ours, theirs or its (when it means belongs to) do not need apostrophes to show possession.
- However, if you want to use 'One's family', you do need an apostrophe.
- There are some pairs of words, one with an apostrophe and one without, which sound the same but have different meanings. Overleaf are some examples.

It's and its

'It's' means 'it is':
> It's sunny outside.

'Its' is a possessive pronoun:
> The dog wants its dinner.

You're and your

'You're' means 'you are':
> You're working hard.

'Your' is a possessive pronoun:
> These are your shoes.

Who's and whose

'Who's means 'who is':
> Who's coming with me?

'Whose' is a possessive pronoun.
> Whose coat is this?

• '60s, 1970s' and 1980s

The apostrophe should only be used to show missing numbers, or possession when it comes to decades. It should never be used for the plural.

> The '60s was an exciting time for music. (Omission)
> 1970s' clothes are back in style. (Possession)
> Personal computers began to be sold in the 1980s. (Plural)

Colon

Colons are used to introduce a list, a long quotation or speech, or an explanation of the first part of a sentence.

Introducing a list – Before the colon, the beginning of the sentence introduces the topic, with each item separated by a comma as follows:

> To punctuate a sentence you can use all, or some, of the following: a full stop, comma, colon, semicolon, apostrophe and speech marks.

Introducing a speech or quotation – The colon is used before the speech or quote in place of a comma.

> *Shakespeare wrote: 'To be, or not to be, that is the question.'*

Introducing an explanation – Colons can link two clauses or sentences where the second explains or draws a conclusion from the first. You do not need a capital letter after the colon:

> *'To be, or not to be, that is the question: whether 'tis nobler in the mind to suffer the slings and arrows of outrageous fortune.'*

> *After looking at the guest list, Alice decided: she was not going to the party.*

Semicolon

Semicolons create a pause that is bigger than a comma but smaller than a full stop.

They can link two sentences which are closely related and could stand alone, although they would then seem rather short or weak. For instance:

The room was silent; no one dared speak a word.

Semicolons can also be used to divide more complex lists where each item is several words long and may already need commas:

For the school trip you will need to take: a waterproof coat and warm sweatshirt; a notepad, pencil and coloured pen; a packed lunch; something to drink; and a small amount of spending money.

Brackets

Brackets (always in pairs) are used to separate extra information or comments from the rest of the sentence. For example:

Purple berries (blueberries, blackcurrants, blackberries and grapes) are packed with antioxidants.

If the bracketed phrase comes at the end of a sentence, you still put the full stop outside the brackets, it only goes inside if the brackets contain a whole sentence:

Purple berries are packed with antioxidants. (Eat a mixture of blueberries, blackcurrants, blackberries and grapes.) This is why they are so good for you.

When a sentence also needs a comma (as in this example), that should also come after the brackets.

Hyphens

Hyphens link words and parts of words, although they are no longer used as widely as they once were.

Compound words – hyphens are used to join two or more words to make a new word, such as mother-in-law and up-to-date.

They can also form compound adjectives:
> *He was a well-known actor.*

But if the adjective comes after the noun it is not hyphenated:
> *The actor was well known.*

To join a prefix – particularly if the prefix ends, and the word begins, with a vowel, for instance: re-elected or co-operate.

Increasingly, the hyphen is being dropped and words like 'cooperate' appear as one word.

Sometimes it helps to use a hyphen. These two sentences have quite different meanings:
> *There were twenty-odd guests at the party.*
> *There were twenty odd guests at the party.*

You can also change the meanings of words:
Use 'resign' to leave a job, and 're-sign' to sign again.
Or, 'recover' to get better, and 're-cover' to cover something again.

Numbers – Hyphens are still used when numbers are written out, for example:

> two-thirds
> thirty-four
> two hundred and fifty-five

Dashes

Dashes can be used instead of colons, semicolons and even commas. They should not be overused but they can help to suggest surprise or other emotions:

> *I opened the door and there they were – all my favourite friends and family.*

Two dashes can work in the same way as brackets:

> *Nothing was safe – shoes, socks, cushions – the puppy would chew them all.*

Writing Style

The right order

As well as choosing the right words, grammar and punctuation, the order in which words are used makes a huge difference to the meaning of a sentence.
For instance:

> *Walking downstairs, the grandfather clock chimed.*

This sounds as if the grandfather clock was walking downstairs chiming. It would make better sense to write:

While I was walking downstairs, the grandfather clock chimed.

The usual order in longer sentences is subject noun, verb, object noun and object noun, for example:
   George glimpsed a fox in the moonlight.

To add variety to a piece of writing, or to introduce an element of suspense or atmosphere, the order can be changed so that the subject noun no longer comes first but the sense is still clear:
   In the moonlight, George glimpsed a fox.

TEACHERS SAY

Encourage children to play around with word order to create different atmospheres or effects in their writing, to think about what sounds more dramatic or exciting. Varying the length of sentences also helps. Short, sharp sentences work best for action, for example:
   The monster hissed. Its shadow crept closer.
   Max turned and ran.

Paragraphs

In written work, sentences are then grouped into paragraphs which essentially develop one subject or idea. It is possible for a paragraph to comprise just one sentence.

Start a new paragraph when the topic changes. For clarity, it is a good idea to leave a line space between paragraphs or to begin with an indent.

Language mnemonics

These are a few traditional mnemonics as a prompt for elements to think about in written work.

Figures of speech
'Most People Sing In Harmony.'
Metaphor, Personification, Simile, Irony, Hyperbole.

Elements of stories
'Very Many Pupils Come to School.'
Viewpoint, Mood, Plot, Characters, Theme, Setting.

Literary genres
Just remember the '3Ps':
Plays, Poetry, Prose.

Ways to improve

The best way to help children improve their writing skills is to encourage them to read. The more they enjoy books and words, the better their own writing style will become. And keep practising. There are lots of opportunities which should not feel like hard work.

Write thank you letters

From an early age, make thank you letters a habit. Relatives will love receiving a written note and it is useful for children to know how to set out a letter.

- They should write their own name and address at the top right-hand corner of their paper.
- Each part of the address should start on a new line.
- Leave a line space below and then write the date.
- Leave a couple of lines space before beginning the letter.

24 High Street,
Anytown,
Middleshire

16 March 2011

Dear Grandma and Grandad,

Thank you for the money that you gave me for my birthday. Mummy and Daddy say I that I must save it for a rainy day.
The man on the television says that it might rain next week!

Yours sincerely,
Jane

- If children are writing a formal letter and do not know the name of the person they are writing to, they should start with 'Dear sir or madam' and finish with 'Yours faithfully'.
- When they know the name of the person to whom they are writing, they can end with 'Yours sincerely'.

Keep a diary

Keeping a diary can be a really good way to write something every day. It will naturally vary according to mood and what has been happening, and challenges the writer to try different styles and vocabulary to match.

- Choose an appealing diary or notebook.
- Add drawings and photos.
- Glue in old tickets and programmes as a record.

PARENTS' TIP

Keeping a daily diary is good practice for school holiday homework when children are often asked to keep a holiday diary.

Ten things to think about when writing a story:

1. Choose what you are going to write about and make a plan.

2. Remember that all stories need a beginning, middle and ending.

3. Set the scene – the opening paragraph should make the reader want to know more.

4. Describe the place where the story takes place.

5. Create an atmosphere that matches the type of story you are writing.

6. Introduce your characters.

7. Give your characters names and personalities. What makes them unique? Describe what they are wearing or what they look like to create a clear image of them.

8. Think about the language and the words you choose. Vary the sentence lengths and adjectives or adverbs to add interest.

9. Are there any amusing, dramatic or interesting events that could be added?

10. The ending – it is vital to have a good ending. This should tie up any loose ends and leave the reader feeling satisfied.

FOUR
SCIENCE

'The important thing in science is not so much to obtain new facts, as to discover new ways of thinking about them,'
SIR WILLIAM BRAGG

'Nothing shocks me. I'm a scientist,'
HARRISON FORD AS INDIANA JONES

Science affects everything we do from the food we eat to the cars we drive and the computers we use. What we are and how we relate to our planet and the universe is underpinned by science. Many of the greatest thinkers from Aristotle to Einstein are scientists, and David Hockney (one of the most important living artists) is now painting on an iPad. Science is part of the everyday, not something separate. Through science we can start to understand our world and provide answers to all those questions that children ask so naturally.

Perhaps the best way to help your child with their science homework is to make it fun. How we apply science defines us and this is increasingly reflected in schools' approach to science teaching. It is broadly divided into three categories covering living things (biology), materials (chemistry) and physical processes (physics).

Food Chains

The interdependence of science and the world is reflected in the interdependence of all living organisms, and one of the most basic ways in which plants and animals depend upon one another is for their food.

Food chains link plants and animals. For instance:
Lettuce leaf eaten by a caterpillar
Caterpillar eaten by a blackbird
Blackbird eaten by a buzzard.

- Plants are at the start of the food chain and are usually very numerous while the animals at the end are fewer in number and much larger in size.
- Plants are **producers** as they make their own food and form the basis of all food chains.
- Animals are **consumers** as they eat other plants and animals.
- Animals can be divided into **herbivores**, which feed on plants, and **carnivores**, which eat other animals.
- Animals can also be divided into **predators** which kill and their **prey**.
- **Scavengers** are carnivores which eat the remains of prey killed by other predators.
- Most plants and animals are part of more than one food chain. For instance: grass is eaten by rabbits which in turn are eaten by foxes; but grass is also eaten by sheep which are eaten by humans; and rabbits might also be eaten by humans or some other predator.
- Changes to one part of the food chain affect every other link, which is important to remember when looking at

humankind's impact on the environment.

- Fungi and bacteria are examples of **decomposers** which break down the remains of plants and animals, releasing chemicals which can be used again, or recycled.

Because most plants and animals are part of more than one food chain, it can be helpful to think in terms of food webs. These also help to reinforce the idea of interdependence and show what might happen if one element disappeared.

For instance, in a food web that included foxes, stoats and birds of prey feeding on insects, mice, small birds and rabbits, which in turn feed on plants, seeds and berries, it is easy to see that if there was another major outbreak of myxomatosis to drastically reduce the number of rabbits, then more mice, small birds and insects would be eaten as a result. Attacks on farm animals such as chickens and young lambs might increase to compensate for the loss of food, and predators might also eat more seeds and fruits leaving fewer of them for other birds. Certain types of plants might increase in number because there would be no longer as many rabbits to crop them.

Plants

Parts of a plant

The petals of flowering plants are usually brightly coloured and
may also be scented to attract insects for pollination. In wind-
or self-pollinated plants, petals are small or non-existent.

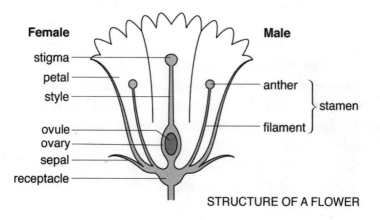

STRUCTURE OF A FLOWER

Sepals – grow in a ring outside the petals. They are often green
or brown and quite small in size. They protect the flower bud.

Nectary – produces sweet nectar which insects drink. The nectaries are usually deep inside the flower which means insects brush past the anthers and pick up pollen grains which they then carry on to the next flower, pollinating it in the process.

Carpel – this is the female part of the flower and it includes the stigma, style and ovary which produces ovules or eggs. This is the part which produces seeds or fruit once pollination has taken place.

Stamen – this is the male part of a plant. Each stamen has a stalk called a filament with an anther containing pollen at the end. Some flowers have many stamens, others just a few. When the anthers or pollen sacs are ripe, they split open to release their pollen.

Receptacle – all parts of a flower are attached to a receptacle at the top of the flower stalk, which is often rounded in shape. In plants such as strawberries, the receptacle grows after fertilization and is edible.

The life cycle of plants

- Pollen is carried by insects or the wind from one flower to another. The stigma has a sticky surface and pollen grains will stick to it during pollination.
- The pollen joins with the ovules, or egg cells, in the ovary to fertilize the plant.
- Fertilization produces seeds or fruit.
- The seeds will grow into new plants after they have been scattered by animals or the wind, in a process called dispersal.

PARENTS' TIP

Look at different flowers to see how they have adapted their shape to attract insects. Bees disappear inside foxgloves, for instance, and you can see the stigma rubbing against their backs.

Did you know?

Most flowers have between five and ten petals. Look at different flowers with your children and try counting them.

Growing plants

A healthy plant needs:

- Light.
- Water.
- Nutrients from the soil (although there are some 'air' plants which rely solely on water).
- Air.
- Warmth, usually from the sun.

1. The roots anchor the plant and take up water and nutrients.
2. The plant's stem carries these nutrients and water to all parts of the plant.
3. The leaves use sunlight, carbon dioxide from the air and water to produce food during photosynthesis. During the process, oxygen is released into the atmosphere.

Grow your own

The easiest and most interesting way to teach children about plants is to actually help them grow some plants from seeds.

- For fast results, try cress or mustard seeds on wet cotton wool or tissue. Children can then eat the results in a sandwich.
- Sunflower seeds are also fun to grow and you can even have a competition to see whose plant grows the tallest.
- Cacti and more unusual plants such as Venus flytraps, or plants with touch-sensitive leaves, can also be interesting to grow and care for.
- Spring bulbs can be grown in either soil or water; these can later be given as a present to grandparents or aunts in home-decorated pots.
- Try varying the amount of light, heat or water to see what works best for your plant.

PARENTS' TIP

Give your child a plant tub or a small area of the garden for them to plant seeds or plants of their choice. Try vegetables or fruit.

You will be surprised at what children will eat if they have helped grow it themselves.

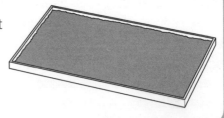

Microorganisms

Microorganisms can only be seen with a microscope. They are all around us – in the air, water and our own bodies. There are three main types:

- Viruses.
- Bacteria.
- Fungi.

When we think of microorganisms, we tend to think of harmful germs spreading diseases and illnesses (like flu or chickenpox which are caused by viruses and can spread very quickly). But there are also helpful microorganisms which are vital for our health and well-being. Here are some examples of harmful and helpful bacteria.

Harmful bacteria can cause:

Food poisoning – through bacteria such as salmonella in uncooked foods like chicken, eggs and meat.
Prevention – make sure food is thoroughly cooked and keep any uncooked meat away from other foods; wash hands before and after food preparation, before meals, and after going to the toilet.

Tooth decay – due to a build-up of dental plaque.
Prevention – regularly clean teeth at least twice a day.

Sore throats – caused by streptococcus bacteria.
Prevention – frequent hand washing and covering your mouth when you cough or sneeze.

PARENTS' TIP

Yeast is an example of a 'friendly' fungus which can be used to make bread and cakes. Try making dough with your child and watching the mixture double in size as the yeast begins to work.

Helpful bacteria

- Bacteria called bacillus are used in the development of antibiotics.
- Lactobacillus are used in the production of yogurt.
- The fermentation process in cheese and beer making relies on bacteria.
- Bacterial decomposers break down plant matter and compost to release nutrients.
- Rhizobium bacteria in the roots of peas and beans convert nitrogen from the air into nitrogen that the plants can use for growth.

Experiment – Spin the egg

You can tell the difference between raw and hard-boiled eggs without cracking the shell: make sure they are the same temperature and try spinning them. The hard-boiled egg will spin but the raw egg will wobble. And if you try to stop the eggs, the raw one will continue to wobble due to inertia.

Habitats

A habitat provides food, shelter and somewhere to live for a group of animals and plants. It could be the small area beneath a stone, a hedgerow, seashore or a vast jungle. Habitats can be any size and can be found anywhere, and the animals and plants that live in them are just as diverse. Plants and creatures adapt to their particular habitat and if conditions change, many find it hard to survive.

Changing seasons

- Look at how habitats change with the seasons.
- What does this mean for the creatures that live within them?
- Collect conkers and chestnuts in the autumn.
- Look at what grows at different times of the year.

PARENTS' TIP

Children love investigating the small worlds they can find in their own garden, parks or the seaside. Look at the insects and bugs under leaves, or the creatures that live in ponds and rock pools. Check wildlife books for any that are unfamiliar and talk about the ways they have adapted to their habitat.

Food and Health

All living things need food, whether plant or animal. Plants make their own food but animals have to eat plants or other animals.

Food is necessary:
- For growth.
- To provide energy – not just to move around, but for all the chemical processes that take place to keep the organism alive.
- To repair any damage.

The human body

Humans must eat a balanced diet and drink plenty of water in order to stay healthy. This should include food from each of the four main food groups:

Carbohydrates – although all food provides us with some energy, carbohydrates (including sugars and starches in foods such as potatoes, bread and rice) are the most readily available source.

Proteins – found in meat, fish, eggs, nuts, milk and cheese, help our bodies repair themselves and build skin, muscle, blood and bones.

Fats – are used to form parts of the cell structure; they are stored as a layer of fat to provide energy and keep us warm. Fats are found in egg yolks, cheese, nuts, seeds, butter, meat and milk.

Vitamins and minerals – are found in a range of food including fruits, vegetables, nuts, fish and milk. Eating a rainbow of fruit and vegetables of every colour will make sure your body has the variety of vitamins and minerals it needs to repair itself and keep your brain working well.

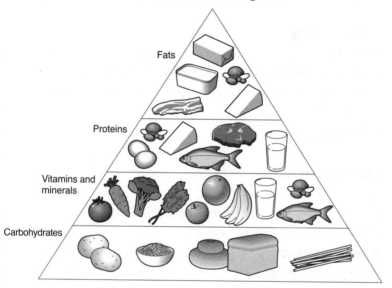

THE FOOD PYRAMID

Did you know?

A calorie is a unit of heat or energy. It measures the amount of heat that would raise the temperature of 1 gram of water by 1°C.

1,000 calories = 1 Kilocalorie or 4.2 joules.

Science spot

A child's skeleton is mainly formed of soft cartilage which gradually transforms into bone. This process is called ossification and bones harden at different ages:

- Elbow at 16.
- Pelvis at 17.
- Ankle at 17.
- Shoulder at 18.
- Knee at 18.
- Wrist at 19.

The heart

The heart is basically a very strong muscle which pumps blood around the body. In humans it has four chambers, two upper and two lower.

- Blood is first pumped to the lungs where it picks up oxygen.
- The pulmonary vein then takes oxygenated blood back to the heart which then pumps it to the rest of the body.
- The pulse is a measure of how fast the heart is beating.
- The pulse can be felt clearly in the neck and groin but it is most easily found in the wrist.
- Use the first two fingers to count the number of pulse beats per minute.

Average heart rates vary among adults; children's hearts generally beat faster, while athletes who are very fit have slower rates.

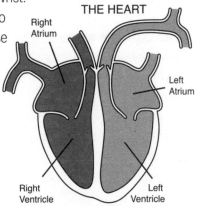

THE HEART

Right Atrium

Left Atrium

Right Ventricle

Left Ventricle

	Average Beats Per Minute
Babies up to 1 year	100–160
Children 1 to 10 years	60–140
10+ to adult	60–100
Top athletes	40–60

Experiment – Test yourself

Check each other's pulse to see how fast your heart is beating. Run up and down the stairs a few times and recheck it, then check again after stopping.

Teeth

Humans have three types of teeth: canines, incisors and molars.

- Incisors and canines bite off food; molars and premolars crush and chew food, making it ready for swallowing.

- Blood vessels supply teeth with oxygen to keep them alive.

- The crown of the tooth is in the mouth; the root is in the jawbone.

- Each tooth has a central pulp cavity, surrounded by layers of cement, dentine and enamel.

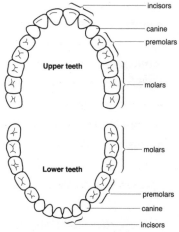

- Tooth decay is caused either by bacteria working on the plaque or by a sugar build-up on teeth.

A young child has around twenty milk teeth; adults have around thirty-two permanent teeth.

Science spot

Look at your pet animals or those you see in parks, farms or at the zoo. Ask children to work out whether they are carnivores, herbivores or omnivores from the shape of their teeth.

The Classification of Living Things

Scientists group plants and animals according to their similarities and differences.

Plants are divided into **flowering** and **non-flowering**.

Animals are divided into **vertebrate** animals (those with a backbone) and **invertebrates** (those without a backbone). Invertebrates include insects and crabs (which have an exoskeleton outside their body), earthworms, molluscs and jellyfish.

There are five classes of vertebrate animals:

Fish Amphibians Reptiles Mammals Birds.

Think of **FARM B** to remember them all.

Did you know?

Roughly 95 per cent of all animals are invertebrates. They tend to be small so we are often less aware of just how many of them there are. Scientists divide invertebrates into over thirty different groups from simple organisms like sea sponges, to insects, spiders, crustaceans and molluscs.

The characteristics of all living things

Whether plant or animal, single- or multi-celled, big or microscopic, all living organisms share seven characteristics:

Movement – single-celled creatures and animals usually move as a whole, while plants and fungi make movements with parts of themselves.

Respiration – food is broken down to provide energy. Most organisms need oxygen for this and so many also breathe, taking in oxygen and giving out carbon dioxide.

Sensitivity – plants and animals are sensitive – or respond – to stimuli.

Growth – this may be a simple increase in size for bacteria or single-celled creatures, but may also involve a growth in the numbers of cells or even a change in shape.

Reproduction – through division, whether that is sexual or asexual reproduction.

Excretion – chemical changes, respiration and nutrition all produce waste products which are then excreted in various ways.

Nutrition – animals take in solid and liquid food, plants create their own food through photosynthesis, and fungi digest and then absorb food.

Generations of schoolchildren remember these through the acronym: **MRS GREN**

Experiment – Test your senses

This can even work as a party game. One person should place a variety of ingredients in separate pots without showing anyone else what they are. Each person takes it in turn to put on a blindfold and then taste each ingredient, guessing what it is. The winner is the person who gets the most ingredients right.

Also test what happens to your sense of taste if you hold your nose.

Another version of this is to have different objects hidden beneath a cloth. Each one is numbered and everyone takes turns to guess the object by touch alone.

Rocks and Soils

When testing soil to find out its age, geologists use this mnemonic to remember the main components:

All Hairy Men Will Buy Razors.

Air, Humus, Mineral salts, Water, Bacteria and Rock particles.

Geological time periods and epochs	Approximate number of years ago
Pre-Cambrian Period	up to 540 million
Cambrian Period	540–505 million
Ordovician Period	505–438 million
Silurian Period	438–408 million
Devonian Period	408–360 million
Carboniferous Period	360–290 million
Permian Period	290–248 million
Triassic Period	248–208 million
Jurassic Period	208–146 million
Cretaceous Period	146–65 million
Tertiary Period:	
Palaeocene Epoch	65–54 million
Eocene Epoch	54–38 million
Oligocene Epoch	38–24 million
Miocene Epoch	24–5 million
Pliocene Epoch	5–1.8 million

Quaternary Period:
    Pleistocene Epoch   1,800,000–10,000
    Recent (Holocene) Epoch   10,000 to the present day

Scientists vary on the exact dates (what's a million years here and there?) but to help remember the correct order, think of these sentences:
Pregnant Camels Often Sit Down Carefully. Perhaps Their Joints Creak? Possibly Early Oiling Might Prevent Painful Rheumatism.

Dinosaurs roamed the Earth during the Cretaceous, Jurassic and Triassic periods, while the first large mammals appeared during the Palaeocene epoch. Australopithecus, an early hominid, first appeared in the Pliocene epoch, and modern humans during the Pleistocene epoch. The Recent or Holocene epoch marked a mass extinction of large mammals and birds, probably at the end of the last Ice Age; it also saw the real beginnings of modern civilization.

Solids, Liquids and Gases

Each has very different properties.

Solids

- Keep their shape and always take up the same volume.
- Can be held and cut.
- Solids such as sand and flour can be poured but they do not flow like liquids.
- May turn into a liquid if they are heated, e.g. chocolate, butter or sugar.
- The temperature at which a solid melts is called the melting point.

Experiment – Melting Chocolate

Time how long it takes for a square of chocolate to melt in different places. Place one square on a plate in the sun, one on top of a radiator, and one in hot milk; you could even see how long they take to melt in the mouth. Once chocolate has melted (assuming it hasn't been eaten), how long does it take for it to solidify?

Liquids

- Change shape but their volume stays the same.
- They flow and can be poured.
- They are not easy to hold.
- Heating a liquid can turn it into a gas, e.g. water evaporates to create steam.
- Cooling a liquid can turn it into a solid, e.g. water freezes to form ice.

Experiment – Melting ice cubes

Pour warm water into a measuring jug and drop in some ice cubes. Wait for them to melt and check what happens to the level of water. You should find that the level remains about the same as when water freezes it takes up more space than it does when liquid.

Gases

- Spread and change shape.
- Can be squashed and their volume can change.
- May be invisible.
- Condense into a liquid when cooled.

Experiment – Expanding air

Blow up a balloon so it is not fully inflated. Stretch it over the top of an empty bottle and then stand the bottle in a pan of hot water. Wait for a few minutes to see what happens. The balloon should continue to inflate as the air heats and expands.

Experiment – Vinegar volcano

You can try this in a container but children may like to build their own volcano for the full effect. Simply mix vinegar with bicarbonate of soda and watch the bubbles erupt. The acid in the vinegar reacts with the bicarbonate of soda to form carbonic acid, which splits into water and carbon dioxide to create the fizzing bubbles.

Force and Motion

Force is measured in Newtons, named after Sir Isaac Newton (1643–1727) who is famous for developing his three laws of motion and his theory of gravity.

Newton's Laws of Motion

The first law of motion is the law of inertia – an object remains at rest or in motion unless an external force acts upon it. For example, a car at the top of a hill will continue rolling downhill unless the handbrake is applied.

The second law – the applied force is equal to the mass of an object multiplied by its acceleration, which is written as $F = ma$.

The third law – for every action there is an equal and opposite reaction. This basically explains what happens when we step from a moving train onto a stationary platform.

Force and motion facts

- Forces are pushes or pulls.
- Gravity is the force that pulls things to the ground on Earth.
- Friction is the force between two surfaces that are moving against each other.
- Friction always slows a moving object. The rougher the surface the greater the friction.
- Friction produces heat, which is why rubbing cold hands together warms them.
- Speed is the rate at which an object moves.
- Velocity is both the speed and direction of a moving object.

Did you know?
Newton was the first scientist to be knighted. As well as his work on motion, gravity, colour and mathematics, he also invented the cat flap.

Light Facts

The speed of light:
- Light travels at almost 300,000 km per second.
- It takes roughly seven seconds for light from the Sun to reach the Earth.
- The speed of light slows as it moves through the atmosphere, through water and diamonds.
- The Sun is an obvious source of light and heat.
- The Moon does not emit light, it reflects it from the sun.

Colours of the rainbow
When white light passes through a prism, it separates into the seven colours of the colour spectrum. These can also been seen in rainbows and they always appear in the same order:

Red Orange Yellow Green Blue Indigo Violet.
An easy way to remember their order is the sentence:
Richard Of York Gave Battle In Vain. Or: *ROY G BIV.*

Did you know?
Dogs really are colour-blind, seeing only shades of grey.

Experiment – Make your own rainbow

Hold a glass of water in front of a sunny window. Place a sheet of white paper beneath it so the sunlight refracts through the water and onto the paper.

Primary and secondary colours

The primary colours of light are blue, green and red, and when combined these three make white light.

Yellow, magenta and cyan are secondary colours, which can be used to make most other shades.

Seeing things

When light hits an object, it bounces off it and this reflected light enters our eyes which is what allows us to see the object.

Electricity

- Electricity is energy.
- It flows through a circuit which must be complete for the current to work.
- All electrical circuits need a power source which can be a small battery, or a large power station; it can also be wind-, solar- or water-powered.
- Electricity travels easily through conductors such as metal or water.

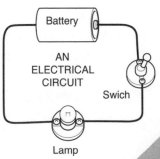

AN ELECTRICAL CIRCUIT

Battery

Swich

Lamp

Did you know?

Lightning is a form of static electricity on a large scale that happens when electrons in the clouds are attracted to protons from the ground.

- As our bodies are 90 per cent water, this means that we make very good conductors.
- Insulators such as plastic, rubber, glass and wood do not conduct electricity, which is why they are used to cover and insulate electrical cables.

Static electricity

Every object is made up of atoms and within each atom are minuscule particles called protons and electrons. Protons carry a positive charge and electrons a negative one. Usually, these two opposing charges cancel one another out but electrons can move causing an imbalance which results in static electricity. One way they can move is through two objects rubbing together, for example, when you pull off a woollen hat, hair can become static and stands on end.

Experiment – Static balloons

Statically charge a balloon by rubbing it against a jumper or hair. It will pick up extra electrons and, when held against a neutral surface, such as a wall or ceiling, will stick to it.

Astronomy

The Earth

The Earth is just one planet in our Solar System. It orbits the Sun at roughly 110,000 km per hour (almost 70,000 miles per hour) and is around 150 million km (93 million miles) away from the Sun. It takes a year to complete one orbit. The Earth also spins on its own axis, an imaginary line running between the North and South Poles, once every 24 hours which is why we have day and night.

The atmosphere

Earth's atmosphere is made up of layers of gases which are kept in place by the Earth's gravity.

- Oxygen makes up about 20 per cent of the atmosphere.
- Nitrogen is roughly 78 per cent.
- Carbon dioxide is 0.0385 per cent.
- Argon is less that 1 per cent.
- Water vapour is usually around 1 per cent.

The different atmospheric strata are:

- **Troposphere** – closest to the Earth. This is where the weather happens.
- **Stratosphere** – this contains the ozone layer and it is also where jets fly.
- **Mesosphere** – meteors usually burn up in this layer.
- **Thermosphere** – this is the biggest layer and the air is very thin here, which means temperatures can vary wildly in response to the Sun's activity but are usually around 1000°C.

Exosphere
Thermosphere
Mesosphere
Stratosphere
Troposphere

- **Exosphere** – there are almost no gases here and this is where weather satellites orbit.

Inside the Earth

- The surface is called the Crust and is made up of separate rocky plates that move and rub against each other which can result in earthquakes.
- The maximum depth of the Crust is 50 km (31 miles).
- The Mantle is the layer below the Crust and this is partly liquid.
- Next lies the Outer Core which is liquid and in constant movement.
- The Inner Core is at the centre of the Earth. This is solid metal, composed largely of iron.
- Mars, Venus and Mercury also have rocky crusts and solid metal cores.

LAYERS OF THE EARTH

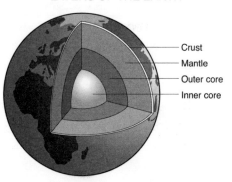

Crust
Mantle
Outer core
Inner core

The Moon

Like the Earth, the Moon is spherical in shape but it is roughly a quarter of the Earth's size. It is 384,400 km (240,250 miles) away and takes 28 days to orbit our planet. Earth's gravity causes the Moon to spin; it takes the same time for it to spin around once as it does for it to orbit the Earth, meaning the same side is always facing us.

Phases of the Moon

The moon does not make its own light, it reflects the Sun's rays. Different proportions of the sunlit side are visible each night as it orbits the Earth. These are known as the phases of the Moon.

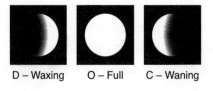

D – Waxing   O – Full   C – Waning

To work out whether the Moon is waxing or waning, remember:

When Coming, the Moon is really departing.
When Departing, it is really coming.

So if there is a left-hand curve to the crescent, it means the Moon is waning or decreasing in size.

A right-hand curve to the crescent means it is waxing or increasing.

The Sun

The Sun is a star which essentially means it is a ball of exploding gas. Atoms of hydrogen join together to form helium. This process of nuclear fusion radiates heat and light. Without this sunshine, there would be no life on Earth.

- The Sun has a diameter of 1.4 million km (875,000 miles).
- Dark, cooler patches, called sunspots, sometimes appear on the Sun's surface.
- These sunspots can sometimes form enormous groups.
- Solar flares are explosions of radiation.
- The Sun's gravity locks everything within a 6,000-million-km (3,730-mile) range into its orbit.
- Solar wind is the stream of charged particles the Sun blows into space.
- Solar winds hit the Earth constantly but are not usually noticeable.
- However, geomagnetic storms can disrupt power grids; when particles are trapped near the North and South Poles they result in the aurora borealis (or northern lights) and the aurora australis (or southern lights).

The Solar System

Following the demotion of Pluto as a planet in 2006, there are now eight planets in our Solar System. Working out from the Sun, they are:

Mercury   *Venus*   *Earth*   *Mars*   *Jupiter*
Saturn   *Uranus*   *Neptune.*

Mercury   Venus   Earth   Mars   Jupiter   Saturn   Uranus   Neptune

To remember them in the correct order, think of the mnemonic:
My Very Educated Mother Just Served Us Noodles.

(With Pluto included, this used to be:
My Very Educated Mother Just Served Us Nine Pies.)

In size order, starting with the largest, they are:
*Jupiter   Saturn   Uranus   Neptune   Earth   Venus
Mars   Mercury.*

You can remember them by:
Jason Sat Under Ninety-Eight Vicious Monster Munchers.

Within the Solar System there are also:
Asteroids – large chunks of rock or rock and metal which orbit the Sun like planets. Most are in the Asteroid Belt, a region between Mars and Jupiter.
Comets – are huge icy masses which are visible when they come briefly close to the Sun. They sometimes have a distinctive tail.
Meteoroids – are small pieces of debris. When they fall they are called meteors. Most burn up in the Earth's atmosphere but any that hit the surface are called meteorites.

Moons – many planets have moons orbiting them, some more than one. Jupiter, for instance, has five major moons (Amalthea, Io, Europa, Ganymede and Callisto), but there are sixty-three others known to astronomers and probably more as yet undiscovered.

Light years

Distances in space are so vast that they are usually measured in light years. One light year is approximately 9.46 million million km (or 5.88 million million miles), which is basically the distance that light travels in a year.

FIVE
THE WORLD

'History is the witness that testifies to the passing of time; it illumines reality, vitalizes memory, provides guidance in daily life and brings us tidings of antiquity,'
CICERO, 106–43 BC

History

History should be one of the most exciting subjects to study: the clue's in the name. History is stories – of people, places, politics, kings, battles, religion, art, buildings, science, technology and much more. Most importantly, it is the story of how ordinary people lived and how times have changed. It shows how the events of the past shape our present and future.

Although history is so much more than facts and figures, it seemed most useful to provide a framework of dates and events here as a starting point from which to find out more. It would also be impossible to cover every single interesting historical character or happening, and there are many specific sources of detailed information available on the Internet and in other history books.

TEACHERS SAY

Help your child to choose an interesting character from history. Encourage them to discover everything they can about their choice. Or take a particular event. What was life like at that time? How is it different from today?

Key dates in world history

Around 3500 BC – three key inventions were made which revolutionized farming, trade and exploration: the wheel and plough were developed in Mesopotamia and the sail was invented in Egypt.

Around 3200 BC – the Sumerians developed a cuneiform system of writing in Mesopotamia using symbols and pictographs. There is some debate over what really is the earliest example of writing. Archaeologists have uncovered other ancient clay tablets in Egypt, China and Pakistan. Some also claim that symbolism was used by cave painters of the Neolithic Age or New Stone Age, beginning around 9500 BC in the Middle East.

3100 BC – the first henge was built at Stonehenge. This was a large earthwork, with a ditch, mound and holes. The Stonehenge we see today was begun around 2150 BC.

2737 BC – tea was discovered by the Chinese Emperor Shen Nung.

2680 BC – the Step Pyramid (the first great pyramid) was built for Pharaoh Djoser at Saqqara.

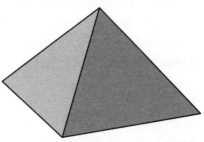

2550 BC – the Great Pyramid of King Khufu was built at Giza. It is the largest stone structure ever built and it is impossible to count all the blocks used in its construction.

Around 1600 BC – Greek civilization began and with it came the modern alphabet and early studies of mathematics, philosophy, medicine and political thought.

Around 1270 BC – Moses led the exodus of the Israelites from Egypt.

Around 1200 BC – iron production began in Anatolia and Europe, although there is some evidence for ironworking as early as 1800 BC in India.

753 BC – Rome was founded. Myth has it that Romulus and Remus – twin descendants of Aeneas who were raised by a wolf – founded the city.

563 BC – the birth of Siddhartha Gautama, the founder of Buddhism.

Around 551 BC – Confucius was born in China.

509 BC – the Roman Republic was established.

507 BC – democracy was established in Athens.

490 BC – the Battle of Marathon took place in which the Greeks defeated an invasion from Persia.

336 BC – Alexander the Great succeeded his father Philip II as king and began a series of campaigns to extend the Macedonian Empire, invading India in 327 BC. He died in Babylon in 323 BC at the age of 32.

Around 300 BC – work began on the Great Wall of China to keep out invading tribes.

Around 105 BC – the Silk Road was opened.

55 BC – Julius Caesar led the first Roman invasion of Britain.

44 BC – Julius Caesar was assassinated by Brutus on the 15, also known as the Ides, of March. He played a key role in the transformation of Rome from a republic into an empire.

27 BC – the Roman Empire was founded and was to last until AD 476 in western Europe. There had been some expansion previously during the Republic but 27 BC marks the start of the empire's classical period.

5 BC – the probable birth year of Jesus Christ.

Around AD 58 – Buddhism arrived in China from India.

AD 79 – Mount Vesuvius erupted burying the cities of Pompeii and Herculaneum.

105 – modern paper was invented in China. Easily and cheaply made, it replaced stone, slate and papyrus.

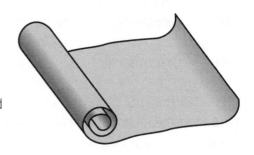

221 – an area resembling modern China was unified under the Qin Dynasty, the first dynasty of Imperial China.

312 – the Roman Emperor Constantine converted to Christianity and Christianity spread across Europe.

450s – Angle and Saxon invaders arrived and settled in Britain.

476 – the Roman Empire fell in the West although it continued in Byzantium (Constantinople) until 1453.

Around 570 – Muhammad was born in Mecca.

711 – the Moors settled in Spain taking over from the Visigoths.

Around 730 – printing was developed in China.

800 – Charlemagne was crowned the first Holy Roman Emperor in western Europe.

860 – the Vikings settled in Iceland.

Around 986 – a Viking colony was established in Greenland under Eric the Red.

Around 1000 – the Viking explorer Leif Ericsson landed on islands off the coast of Canada and finally in Newfoundland.

1002 – Leif's brother Thorwald established a colony.

1054 – the schism between the Greek and Latin Christian Churches permanently divided Christianity.

1066 – the Battle of Hastings. William the Conqueror led the Norman Conquest – the last invasion of Britain.

1088 – the world's first university was founded in Bologna in Italy.

1096 – the first crusade was launched against Muslims in Palestine.

1206 – Genghis Khan began his conquest of Asia.

1215 – Genghis Khan captured Beijing and established Mongol rule.

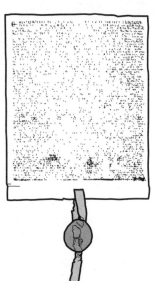

1215 – Magna Carta was signed by King John at Runnymede. For the first time the king's power was constrained. This is generally regarded as the beginning of the modern idea of constitutional law and was influential in the development of democracy.

1220 – foundation of the Inca civilization in Peru.

1227 – the death of Genghis Khan.

1240 – Mongols captured Kiev in Russia.

1271 – Marco Polo travelled to Asia and China, returning to his home city of Venice 24 years later in 1295.

1325 – in Central America the Aztecs built Tenochtitlán which is now Mexico City.

1337 – the Hundred Years War began between England and France. It ended in 1453.

1347 – the Black Death arrived in Europe from Asia. The plague swept through the continent wiping out over a quarter of the population, some 25 million people. Its impact had a lasting effect on the social and political order, as well as on religious thought, art and literature.

1368 – the Ming Dynasty was founded in China and the Mongols were driven out.

1382–4 – John Wycliffe translated the Bible into English.

1387–1400 – Geoffrey Chaucer wrote *The Canterbury Tales*.

1420 – the Chinese rounded the Cape of Good Hope.

1450–5 – Johannes Gutenberg developed a mechanical printing press with movable type. The Gutenberg Bible was the first major book to be printed. This marked a revolution in the way books were produced and ushered in the age of print. Just twenty-one complete copies of the Gutenberg Bible are known to survive.

1453 – Constantinople fell to the Ottoman Turks led by Muhammad II. This marked the end of the Roman Empire in the East. Nearly 500 years of Turkish domination of the eastern Mediterranean, the Middle East and North Africa followed.

1469 – Aragon and Castile in Spain were unified through the marriage of Ferdinand, King of Aragon, and Isabella, Queen of Castile.

1485 – Richard III was defeated by Henry VII at the Battle of Bosworth Field. This marked the end of the Plantagenet and the start of the Tudor dynasty. It was the penultimate battle of the Wars of the Roses.

1492 – Christopher Columbus discovered the New World, landing in the Bahamas on 12 October. He did not actually reach the mainland until his third voyage in 1498 when he landed in South America.

1497 – Vasco da Gama sailed from Portugal to India.

1502 – the first African slaves arrived in the Spanish colonies in America. Slaves were first introduced to Virginia in North America in 1619.

1504–8 – Peter Henlein invented the first watch in Germany. It was portable but not very accurate. Patek Philippe is usually credited with making the first wristwatch in the late 1900s, although this was only worn by women.

1508–12 – Michelangelo painted the ceiling of the Sistine Chapel in Rome.

1517 – Martin Luther nailed his Ninety-Five Theses to the door of All Saints' Church in Wittenberg, launching the Reformation and the beginnings of Protestantism.

1519–20 – Cortés began his conquest of Mexico and captured the Aztec capital of Tenochtitlán.

1520 – Cortés introduced chocolate to Spain. Columbus had tasted it first but dismissed its importance. The year 1585 saw the first large commercial shipment of chocolate from Veracruz, Mexico, to Seville in Spain. It was not until 1657 that the first chocolate house opened in London.

1532 – the Spanish conquistadors discovered potatoes growing in the high Andes. They were not introduced to Europe until the second half of the sixteenth century.

1534 – Henry VIII was declared head of the newly established Church of England through the Act of Supremacy.

1543 – Copernicus stated that the Earth revolves around the Sun.

1564 – on 23 April (St George's Day), William Shakespeare was born in Stratford upon Avon.

1576 – Martin Frobisher left England on the first of three voyages in search of the Northwest Passage.

1583 – the first British settlement was established in Newfoundland, North America.

1588 – the Spanish Armada was defeated by the English navy.

1605 – the Gunpowder Plot to blow up the English Houses of Parliament was foiled. Guy Fawkes and the other plotters are still remembered on 5 November.

1607 – the first permanent British colony in North America was founded in Jamestown, Virginia.

1609–10 – Henry Hudson set off in search of the Northwest Passage.

1611 – the King James Bible was published.

1620 – the Pilgrim Fathers set sail for the New World in the Mayflower. They landed in Cape Cod and set up a colony in Plymouth, Massachusetts.

1642–51 – English Civil War.

1649 – Charles I was executed.

1649–60 – Commonwealth of England.

1653–8 – Oliver Cromwell was Lord Protector of the Commonwealth of England.

1660 – Restoration of the monarchy. Charles II was proclaimed King of Britain.

1666 – the Great Fire of London destroyed much of the medieval city.

1676 – in Denmark, Ole Rømer calculated the speed of light.

1678–82 – Robert de la Salle travelled across North America.

1685 – a great year for music with the births of Bach, Handel and Rameau.

1687 – Sir Isaac Newton published *Philosophiæ Naturalis Principia Mathematica* (Mathematical Principles of Natural Philosophy), which described universal gravitation and the three laws of motion.

1756 – Wolfgang Amadeus Mozart was born on 27 January.

1767 – the invention of the Spinning Jenny and mechanization of weaving signalled the beginning of the Industrial Revolution.

1769 – James Cook sailed to Tahiti in the *Endeavour* and discovered the east coast of New Zealand.

1770 – Cook landed in Botany Bay, Australia.

1770 – Ludwig Van Beethoven was born in Bonn, Germany.

1775 – the American War of Independence began with the rebellion of the thirteen original colonies. It finally ended in 1783 with the Treaty of Paris.

1776 – the American Declaration of Independence was made on 4 July.

1779 – Cook sailed to the Sandwich Islands in Hawaii where he was killed.

1787 – the Founding Fathers set out the principles of the American Constitution. It is not only the oldest, but also the shortest, national constitution still in use today.

1789 – the French Revolution overthrew the monarchy and established a republic. The year 1789, on 14 July, saw the storming of the Bastille in Paris; Louis XVI and Marie Antoinette were guillotined in 1793 – the year 1793 also saw the start of the Reign of Terror. Napoleon became First Consul in 1799 and Emperor in December 1804.

1795 – George Bass and Matthew Flinders made the first expedition inland from the eastern coast of Australia.

1796 – Edward Jenner successfully vaccinated against smallpox.

1805 – on 21 October Admiral Lord Nelson was killed at the Battle of Trafalgar where Napoleon was defeated.

1807 – abolition of the slave trade in Britain. Slavery itself was not made illegal until the Abolition of Slavery Act of 1833.

1814 – the Battle of New Orleans, the last battle of the 1812 war between the US and Britain. Andrew Jackson finally defeated the invading British army in January 1815.

1815 – the Battle of Waterloo on 18 June marked the final defeat of Napoleon and the end of his empire.

1829 – Stephenson's *Rocket* was built for the Manchester and Liverpool Railway, heralding the start of steam railways and cheap, fast travel.

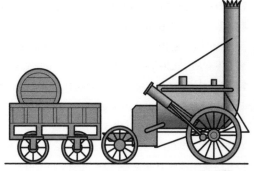

1831 – Charles Darwin sets sail on HMS *Beagle* bound for South America. Leaving on 27 December, the voyage lasted for almost 5 years.

1833 – Abolition of Slavery Act by the British Government.

1839–42 – the First Opium War between Britain and China.

1842 – settlement of the Opium War cedes Hong Kong to Britain.

1845–52 – the Great Famine in Ireland. Robert Peel repealed the Corn Laws ushering in free trade; mass emigration from Ireland to the US began.

1848 – the year of revolutions in Europe. Karl Marx and Friedrich Engels published *The Communist Manifesto*.

1850–64 – Taiping Rebellion in southern China against the ruling Qing Dynasty, the last dynasty of Imperial China.

1853–6 – the Crimean War. Florence Nightingale's work there began a more modern approach to nursing and hospitals. The first war correspondent reported from the front line.

1859 – Darwin's *The Origin of Species*, outlining his theory of evolution, was published by John Murray.

1861–2 – John Stuart completed his crossing of Australia.

1861–5 – the American Civil War was fought between eleven Southern Confederate States and the victorious Union.

1863 – work began on the London Underground.

1875 – Alexander Graham Bell invented the telephone and Henry Nestlé, along with Daniel Peter, invented milk chocolate.

1876 – General Custer made his famous last stand against the Sioux at the Battle of the Little Bighorn.

1885 – the world's first skyscraper, the Home Insurance Building, was built in Chicago.

1885 – Karl Benz developed the first petrol engine car.

1893 – New Zealand was the first nation to introduce full women's suffrage. The vote was granted to women in Great Britain in 1918, followed by the US in 1920.

1898 – Pierre and Marie Curie discovered radium.

1903 – on 17 December, the Wright brothers made the world's first successful flight from Kill Devil Hills in North Carolina.

1905–16 – Albert Einstein published his papers on the *Theory of Relativity*.

1909 – Robert Peary, an engineer in the US navy, and Matthew Henson claimed to have reached the North Pole, beating the Norwegian Roald Amundsen.

1911 – Amundsen beat Robert Falcon Scott to become the first person to reach the South Pole.

1912 – Scott and four other explorers reached the South Pole in January and died of the cold in February.

1912 – on 14 April the unsinkable ship RMS *Titanic* was hit by an iceberg and sank.

1912 – Automat, the first ever fast-food outlet, opened in New York.

1914–18 – the First World War was fought in Europe. The end of the war saw the collapse of the Habsburg, Ottoman and German empires, and a redrawing of the maps of Europe and the Middle East.

1917 – the Russian Revolution overthrew the Tsar and established a revolutionary state.

1919 – Mahatma Gandhi began his campaign against British rule in India.

1922 – Howard Carter uncovered Tutankhamen's tomb, almost intact, in the Valley of the Kings near Thebes on the River Nile.

1925 – Colonel Fawcett set off across Brazil in search of El Dorado. He was never seen again.

1926 – John Logie Baird invented the television and gave the first public demonstration.

1929 – the Wall Street Crash marked the beginning of the Great Depression.

1933 – Hitler became Chancellor of Germany.

1936–9 – civil war in Spain. General Franco was appointed Head of State.

1937–45 – Chinese–Japanese war.

1938 – Laszlo Biro invented the first ballpoint pen in Hungary.

1939–45 – the Second World War was fought.

1945 – detonation of the atomic nuclear bomb at Hiroshima and Nagasaki.

1945 – Ho Chi Minh announced Vietnamese independence.

1945 – on 24 October the United Nations officially came into existence after the ratification of the UN Charter.

1946–9 – civil war in Greece was fought between communists and royalists.

1947 – Indian Independence saw the partition of the continent into India and Pakistan.

1948 – the State of Israel was declared.

1949 – the Communist People's Republic of China was founded by Chairman Mao.

1950–3 – the Korean War.

1955 – Martin Luther King led the Civil Rights Movement in the US in the Montgomery Bus Boycott.

1957 – Russia launched the first space satellite, *Sputnik 1*.

1958–9 – the silicon chip was invented by Jack Kilby and Robert Noyce. The computer age begins.

1961 – the Russian astronaut Yuri Gagarin became the first person to travel in space.

1961 – the Berlin Wall was built dividing East and West Berlin. It was finally knocked down in 1990.

1963 – President Kennedy was assassinated in Dallas, Texas, on 22 November. He was the youngest president to be elected and spent just over 1,000 days in office.

1968 – Martin Luther King was assassinated on 4 April in Memphis, Tennessee.

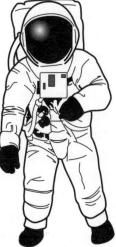

1969 – *Apollo 11* was launched by the US and Neil Armstrong became the first man to walk on the Moon, Buzz Aldrin, the second.

1989–90 – Communist regimes in Europe collapsed with the dissolution of the USSR.

1993 – the European Union was established on 1 November through the Maastricht Treaty.

1994 – Apartheid ended in South Africa and Nelson Mandela was elected President.

2001 – on 11 September, in an act of terrorism, two planes flew into the twin towers of the World Trade Center in New York.

PARENTS' TIP

History can seem much more real if you look at paintings and artefacts. Visit museums and galleries, or historic buildings. Focus on specific historical times or particular people who will appeal to your child.

Kings and Queens of England

House of Wessex

Egbert 827–39
Ethelwulf 839–58
Ethelbald 858–60
Ethelbert 860–5
Ethelred I 865–71
Alfred the Great 871–99
Edward the Elder 899–924
Athelstan 924–39
Edmund I the Magnificent 939–46
Eadred 946–55
Eadwig the Fair 955–9
Edgar the Peaceable 959–75
Edward the Martyr 975–8
Ethelred II the Unready 978–1016
Edmund II Ironside 1016

Danish Line

Canute 1016–35
Harold I (son of Canute) 1035–40
Hardicanute 1040–2

House of Wessex Restored

Edward the Confessor 1042–66
Harold II 1066

House of Normandy

William I the Conqueror 1066–87

William II Rufus 1087–1100
Henry I 1100–35
Stephen 1135–54

Plantagenet House of Angevin

Henry II 1154–89
Richard I the Lionheart 1189–99
John 1199–1216
Henry III 1216–72
Edward I Longshanks 1272–1307
Edward II 1307–27
Edward III 1327–77
Richard II 1377–99

Plantagenet House of Lancaster

Henry IV 1399–1413
Henry V 1413–22
Henry VI 1422–61, 1470–1

Plantagenet House of York

Edward IV 1461–70, 1471–83
Edward V (for 4 months) 1483
Richard III 1483–5

House of Tudor

Henry VII 1485–1509
Henry VIII 1509–47
Edward VI 1547–53
Lady Jane Grey (for 9 days) 1553
Mary I 1553–8
Elizabeth I 1558–1603

House of Stuart

James I (VI of Scotland) 1603–25
Charles I 1625–49

The Commonwealth 1649–60

Oliver Cromwell, Lord Protector 1653–58
Richard Cromwell, Lord Protector 1658–9

House of Stuart Restored

Charles II 1660–85
James II 1685–8

House of Orange and Stuart

William III and Mary II 1689–1702
Anne 1702–14

House of Hanover

George I 1714–27
George II 1727–60
George III 1760–1820
George IV 1820–30
William IV 1830–7
Victoria 1837–1901

House of Saxe-Coburg-Gotha

Edward VII 1901–10

House of Windsor (from 1917)

George V 1910–36
Edward VIII (11 months, abdicated on 10 December) 1936
George VI 1936–52
Elizabeth II 1952–present

Classic Tricks and Rhymes

There are some suitably historic rhymes and mnemonics
which have helped schoolchildren remember significant dates
and facts for decades.

Historic ages

Pupils Eat Grapes Regularly During Morning
Registration In Toilets
Prehistoric, Egyptian, Greek, Roman, Dark Ages, Medieval,
Renaissance, Industrial revolution, Twentieth century and
beyond.

The Seven Wonders of the Ancient World

This verse by Ebenezer Cobham Brewer is over 100 years old.

The Pyramids first, which in Egypt were laid;
Then Babylon's Gardens, for Amytis made;
Third, Mausolus's Tomb, of affection and guilt;
Fourth, the Temple of Dian, in Ephesus built;
Fifth, Colossus of Rhodes, cast in bronze, to the sun;
Sixth, Jupiter's Statue, by Philidas done;
The Pharos of Egypt, last wonder of old,
Or the Palace of Cyrus, cemented with gold.

1. The Great Pyramid of Giza.
2. The Hanging Gardens of Babylon in Baghdad.
3. The Tomb of Mausolus at Halicarnassus in Greece.
4. The Temple of Diana at Ephesus.
5. The Colossus of Rhodes.
6. The Statue of Jupiter at Olympia.
7. The Lighthouse, or Pharos, at Alexandria.

The only Wonder that survives today is the Great Pyramid at Giza in Egypt.

PARENTS' TIP

Live, or rather eat, like a Roman. Create a meal with a Roman theme. Foods such as fish sauce, honey, pine nuts, vinegar, oil and spices (including cinnamon, cumin, nutmeg and allspice) were all common ingredients. Yes, the Romans did farm dormice to eat but you can easily substitute these with chicken thighs and marinade in a mixture of oil, vinegar and spices. The Romans also liked desserts, serving a version of cheesecake made with curd and sweetened with honey. If you're stuck for inspiration, the ancient Roman cook Apicius' recipe book is still available to buy today. You could even dress up for the occasion!

Royal dynasties

No Plan Like Yours To Study History Suitably Well.

Normans, Plantagenets, Lancastrians, Yorkists, Tudors, Stuarts, Hanoverians, Saxe-Coburg and Gotha, Windsor.

King John of Magna Carta fame

Lackland John was a right royal tartar,
Til he made his mark on Magna Carta.
Ink, seal and paper on Runnymede Green
In Anno Domini twelve fifteen.

Columbus's discovery of the New World

In fourteen hundred and ninety-two,
Columbus sailed the oceans blue.

Henry VIII's wives

Divorced, beheaded, died.
Divorced, beheaded, survived.

Or:
Kate and Anne and Jane,
And Anne and Kate again, again.

Catherine of Aragon (1485–1536) married in 1509.
Anne Boleyn (c.1507–1536) married in 1533.
Jane Seymour (1509–1537) married in 1536.
Anne of Cleves (1515–1557) married in 1540.
Kathryn Howard (1521–1542) married in 1540.
Katherine Parr (1512–1548) married in 1543.

The Fire of London

In sixteen hundred and six-six,
London burned like rotten sticks.

The thirteen original colonies of the United States

Carrie Doesn't Give My Mom's Nutty New Noisy
Neighbour Pam Rides In Susie's Van.

Connecticut, Delaware, Georgia, Massachusetts, Maryland, New Hampshire, New York, New Jersey, North Carolina, Pennsylvania, Rhode Island, South Carolina, Virginia.

The Founding Fathers of the US

Will Adam Join Frank Helping Make Jam.

George Washington, John Adams, Thomas Jefferson, Benjamin Franklin, Alexander Hamilton, James Madison, John Jay.

Presidents carved on Mount Rushmore

We Just Like Rushmore.

George Washington, Thomas Jefferson, Abraham Lincoln, Theodore Roosevelt.

Geography

*'Mathematics was hard, dull work.
Geography pleased me more,'*
JOHN JAMES AUDUBON

Geography is the study of the world in which we live: its landscapes, climates, places and environments. It is also the study of people and the way we affect our world. Like history, geography is so much more than just facts and figures but, again, it helps to have some facts on which to build a greater understanding.

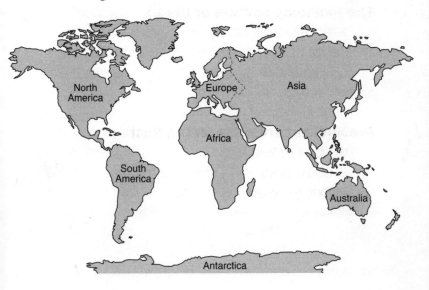

The oceans

There are officially four oceans: Indian, Arctic, Atlantic and Pacific. However, occasionally, the Southern Ocean is included. Also, it could be claimed that the Arctic Ocean is really part of the Atlantic Ocean.

And although everyone knows the phrase, 'sail the seven seas', there are many more than seven in the world.

The ten largest seas

1. **South China** – between Asia and the Philippines.
2. **Caribbean** – to the east of Central America.
3. **Mediterranean** – between Africa and Europe.
4. **Bering** – between Alaska and Russia, to the north of the Pacific and south of the Arctic Oceans.
5. **Gulf of Mexico** – to the east of Mexico, south of the south-eastern states of the US.
6. **Sea of Okhotsk** – north of the Sea of Japan, to the east of Russia and west of the Bering Sea.
7. **East China and Yellow Sea** – east of China, between the Sea of Okhotsk to the north and South China Sea to the south.
8. **Hudson Bay** – Canada, to the west of the Labrador Sea.
9. **Sea of Japan** – between Japan and eastern Asia, south of the Sea of Okhotsk and north of the East China and Yellow Seas.
10. **North** – to the east of Great Britain and west of Denmark.

Did you know?
The deepest valley in the world is the Mariana Trench, beneath the Pacific Ocean, to the east of the Philippines. It is about 10.91 km at its deepest point at Challenger Deep. To give some idea of its scale, the Trench is over 2,000 m deeper than Mount Everest is high.

The world's longest rivers

There is some debate on this according to what is regarded as a river's course and its tributaries, but the acronym **NAMMI YACH-Y** is useful for remembering:

Nile (Egypt)
Amazon (Brazil) – the largest by volume
Mississippi-Missouri (USA) – as a combined river system
Irtysh (Russia)
Yangtze (China)
Amur (Russia)
Congo (Zaire/Congo)
Huang-He or Yellow River (China)

A more accurate list of the world's ten longest rivers, though, is this:

1. **Nile** (Egypt) 6,670 km
2. **Amazon** (Brazil) 6,400 km
3. **Yangtze** (China) 6,380 km
4. **Mississippi-Missouri** (USA) 6,275 km

5. **Yenisei-Angara** (Russia) 5,539 km
6. **Huang-He or Yellow River** (China) 5,464 km
7. **Ob-Irtysh** (Russia) 5,410 km
8. **Parana-Plata** (Argentina) 4,880 km
9. **Congo or Zaire** (Zaire/Congo) 4,700 km
10. **Mekong** (Vietnam/Cambodia) 4,500   km

Continents of the world

There are no strict criteria for defining a continent but the world is generally divided into seven continents. Starting with the largest, these are:

1. **Asia**
2. **Africa**
3. **North America**
4. **South America**
5. **Antarctica**
6. **Europe**
7. **Australia**

Did you know?

Greenland, at 2,166,086 km^2, is the world's largest island. Australia, although also an island, is considered to be the smallest continent, covering a total of 7,686,850 km^2.

Islands are often regarded as part of the nearest continent, so for example, Great Britain and Iceland become part of Europe, while Madagascar is part of Africa.

Some geographers group Australia together with other Pacific islands such as Oceania.

The highest mountains

The mountains of the world have been formed and weathered over millennia through movement of the tectonic plates, volcanic eruptions and glaciation. A mountain must be more than 600 m high, otherwise it is classified as a hill.

The ten tallest mountains are all in the Himalayas:

1. **Everest** (China/Nepal) 8,850 m
2. **K2** (China/Pakistan) 8,611 m
3. **Kanchenjunga** (India/Nepal) 8,586 m
4. **Lhotse** (China/Nepal) 8,516 m
5. **Makalu** (China/Nepal) 8,481 m
6. **Cho Oyu** (China/Nepal) 8,201 m
7. **Dhaulagiri** (Nepal) 8,172 m
8. **Manaslu** (Nepal) 8,156 m
9. **Nanga Parbat** (Pakistan) 8,126 m
10. **Annapurna** (Nepal) 8,078 m

There are a further twenty-three peaks, all over 7,000 m high, and they are all in Asia.

The highest mountains on the other continents are:
South America – Aconcagua (Argentina) 6,960 m
North America – McKinley (Alaska, USA) 6,194 m
Africa – Kilimanjaro (Tanzania) 5,895 m
Antarctica – Vinson Massif 4,897 m
Europe – Mont Blanc (France/Italy) 4,811 m
Oceania – Wilhelm (Papua New Guinea) 4,508 m

The most active volcanoes

Volcanoes are generally found on fault lines in the Earth's crust where tectonic plates are diverging (moving away from each other) or converging (rubbing together). They form a rupture or opening through which lava, or molten rock, ash and gas escape from below the surface. The level of activity varies from week to week but these three volcanoes have been erupting continuously for the greatest periods of time:

Mount Etna in Sicily. This is the largest volcano in Europe and has been erupting for over 3,000 years. On average, it is 3,350 m high but the height varies after each eruption. The most recent one was an ash eruption in April 2010.

Stromboli, one of the Aeolian Islands off the north coast of Sicily, is a volcanic island which has been constantly erupting for over 2,000 years, although each eruption is usually small and at the very summit. The last big eruption was in 2008 when all 700 island inhabitants fled. It stands 926 m above sea level but there are an extra 2,000 m beneath the sea.

Mount Yasur in the South West Pacific is one of 83 islands on the Pacific Ring of Fire. It has been constantly erupting for the last 800 years. It was originally discovered by Captain Cook in 1774 and stands 361 m above sea level.

The volcanoes that produce the most lava are:

- **Kilauea** in Hawaii.
- **Etna** in Italy.
- **Piton de la Fournaise** in La Réunion.
- **Nyamuragira** in the Democratic Republic of Congo.

Weather and climate
- Weather describes the air conditions (the temperature, air pressure, moisture levels, cloudiness or sunshine) in a particular place on a particular day.
- Climate refers to the average – or usual – weather conditions in a place over a long period of time.

Water cycle
The water or hydrologic cycle is the continuous movement of water between the Earth and the atmosphere.
- Water evaporates from oceans, seas and freshwater sources.
- It also moves from plants through transpiration.
- Heat from the sun causes water to evaporate into the air where it condenses into clouds.
- It falls back to Earth as precipitation in the form of rain, snow, sleet or hail.
- And the cycle begins again.

THE WATER CYCLE

Global warming

- At its most basic, global warming is the rising temperature of the Earth's atmosphere.
- The world is expected to be more than 6°C warmer in 80 years time.
- The Earth's atmosphere is made up of layers of gases.
- Greenhouse gases in the atmosphere are responsible for regulating the temperature on the Earth's surface.
- They trap some of the heat from the Sun rather than allowing it to reflect straight back into space, keeping the Earth's temperature at a steady 16°C.
- Without greenhouse gases, the Earth would be extremely cold – around -23°C, which would be too cold for crops to grow and for people and animals to thrive.
- The problem is that the balance is now being upset by humankind's activities.
- We are producing greenhouse gases such as carbon dioxide and methane, which means that too much heat is being stored in the atmosphere.
- In addition, atmospheric pollutants including CFCs (chlorofluorocarbons) and other chemicals are damaging the ozone layer.
- The ozone layer is the layer of ozone gas, a type of oxygen, high in the stratosphere which filters out harmful rays of UVB radiation from sunlight.
- The ozone layer has thinned to such an extent that a hole in the ozone layer over the Antarctic now appears for two or three months every winter, recovering to a certain degree in the spring.

Fossil fuels

Coal, gas and oil are all fossil fuels. They were formed in sedimentary rocks millions of years ago from the remains of plants and animals. Carbon was trapped as these fuels were fossilized, and when they are now burned or used to release energy, carbon dioxide is released back into the atmosphere. We are burning fossil fuels at such a rate that more carbon dioxide is produced than can be absorbed by natural processes (for instance through forests' photosynthesizing). This extra carbon adds to the negative effects of the greenhouse gases.

Possible effects of global warming

- Glaciers and sea ice could melt raising sea levels.
- The oceans absorb more heat than the land and as water expands when heated, this would also add to rising sea levels.
- Coastal areas would flood if sea levels rise.
- Many cities and habitats would be destroyed.
- Climate will change – some countries will become hotter and drier.
- Rainfall will fail leading to droughts, crop failures and famine.
- Extreme weather will become more commonplace with a rise in hurricanes, tornadoes and tsunamis because of changes in heat and water evaporation.

- The thinning of the ozone layer will increase UVB exposure.
- This will increase the risk of skin cancer, cataracts and weakened or suppressed immune systems in people.
- Aquatic ecosystems and plant life will also be damaged as a result of increased UVB radiation.

What is being done?

- The UN Earth Summit meets every 5 years to agree on policy to reduce carbon emissions.
- The Kyoto Protocol on climate change was adopted in 1997 and came into force in 2005.
- Under the terms of Kyoto, countries must meet their targets on reducing greenhouse gas (GHG) emissions.

What can we do to help?

- Be aware of how we use resources.
- Recycle as much as possible – most councils now have recycling schemes for glass, plastic and paper.
- Reuse plastic bags and envelopes.
- Recycle clothes and don't always buy new ones.
- Switch off lights and electrical appliances.
- Avoid leaving televisions and such like on standby.
- Save water and electricity by only filling the kettle with what you need.
- Don't leave the tap running while you brush your teeth – it wastes a staggering amount of water.
- Report leaking mains pipes to your local authority.
- Showering rather than taking a bath uses less water.
- Walk or cycle instead of driving.
- Walk to school, if possible, or at least share lifts.

- Use a cooler wash programme on the washing machine and dishwasher. Clothes will last longer too!
- Start a compost heap in the garden.
- Grow your own vegetables and fruit.
- Eat seasonally and try to choose local food as far as possible to save on air miles.

Alternate forms of energy

- Wind power – is cheap and renewable but protesters claim wind turbines are ugly and damage birdlife. Capacity has increased dramatically in recent years and now wind power accounts for roughly 2 per cent of world electricity.
- Hydro-electricity – generates around 20 per cent of electricity globally but only 2 per cent in the UK.
- Solar power – particularly in sunnier parts of the world this has great potential but at present supplies less than 0.02 per cent of global energy.
- Scientists are constantly looking into ways of creating new environmentally friendly electricity, for example from gases produced from landfill sites or plant fuels.

SIX
WAYS OF LEARNING

'Tell me and I'll forget; show me and I may remember; involve me and I'll understand,'
CHINESE PROVERB

ICT

ICT stands for Information and Communications Technology and basically covers any device that can store and transmit information, from computers, digital televisions and radios, to mobile phones. Just as we increasingly rely on all forms of ICT in our everyday lives and businesses, so schools are placing a growing emphasis on ICT to support pupils' work in all subjects. You don't have to be a computer wizard to help your child with this. Key skills to encourage, include:

- Talking about what information your child needs for a particular piece of work.
- Looking at all the different sources they might use.
- Checking information for accuracy, particularly facts found on the Internet.
- Comparing different sources, for instance the Internet, books and newspapers, even television and film.
- It's really useful for children to get used to using lots of different types of source material to gather information; some will naturally appeal more than others.

- Helping your child's understanding by looking at the material they have found.
- Talking about what is relevant, checking facts and encouraging them to think about what else they might need to find out.

Unlike when most parents were at school, it is almost too easy to find information today and this can cause its own problems. An important aspect of your child's homework will be learning how to spot what is relevant, develop ideas and organize the information before preparing a clear and attractive piece of work.

Not only do children need to know how to find information, they also need to know how to present it in different forms, deciding what works best. It may be:

- a simple piece of written work,
- but it could be a poster,
- picture, or
- prepared speech, or
- a computer-generated presentation complete with graphics and sound effects.

179

Think about

- The purpose of the piece and who it is aimed at.
- Layout – what would be the clearest and most appealing.
- The most appropriate typefaces to use.
- Pictures to include – drawings or photos.
- Tables or graphs for facts.
- Graphics.
- Sound effects.

Children often have to work with others to develop ideas and may be asked to share information by e-mail or evaluate each other's work.

Podcasts

- Podcasts are different from audio recording.
- Think of them as chapters in a book.
- Children learn how to record and edit sounds.
- Many schools now encourage children to record and broadcast podcasts on all sorts of subjects with different themes.
- Children are involved and come up with lots of ideas about what to include.
- Creating their own podcast can help with speaking and listening skills, research, and also makes children think about exactly what will appeal to an audience.
- The recordings are uploaded and turned into a feed which other pupils and parents – sometimes even members of the public – sign up to receive.

TEACHERS SAY

Most schools now have their own Intranets. Pupils will be given a password to access this, both at school and at home. Day-to-day school information and newsletters, as well as specific class homework, revision games and notes are often included.

Some schools also subscribe to learning websites, which pupils can again access using their password and school's login, for example:

Linguascope is an excellent language website offering listening exercises, word searches and games in modern foreign languages at different levels. MyMaths even offers online homework tasks for various stages. Both sites are useful for parents, as well as children.

Increasingly, children will be expected to access such sites for homework.

- You just need a simple recording device to start – children can even use a mobile phone.
- There are many easy-to-follow, free programs on the Internet to help children create their own podcast.
- They can even add music (providing copyright is cleared).

Preparing for the Next Stage

As your child grows older and progresses through school, there will increasingly be times when they need to memorize and revise what they have learned. This is so that learning sticks for the sake of their general knowledge and education, but also so that children can prepare for tests and exams.

Ways to learn

It's really important to remember that everyone learns differently and at their own pace. What is easy for one child will be hard for someone else. The key is to help your child find out what works best for them and how to play to their strengths. For most, it will involve a combination of approaches.

Remember: **See, Hear, Say, Do** is best for learning.

For general note-taking

1. Read through carefully and take notes.
2. Read and condense the notes.
3. Try to memorize the notes.
4. Review what's been learned.
5. Read through and retest at regular intervals.

When learning a foreign language

- Try recording vocabulary.
- You could even record questions to answer.

If your child generally enjoys linguistics and words, and likes reading and writing, encourage them to:

- Form questions from their notes.
- Find and write out the answers, and repeat them aloud.
- Describe what they are learning out loud.
- Summarize a topic in their own words.
- Devise their own mnemonics to prompt their memory.
- Record summaries to play back.

If your child is very logical, enjoying numbers and maths, suggest they:

- List and number the main points in sequence.
- Order information as far as possible.
- Devise their own timeline of facts.
- Make use of diagrams and charts.

For children who respond to pictures and visual stimuli, suggest they:

- Use mind maps and spider diagrams (see page 185).
- Create a strong visual image to accompany their notes.
- Devise a poster of information.
- Use colour and different typefaces to highlight key points.
- Circle key words and rewrite them.
- Watch any relevant films or documentaries on the subject.
- Encourage them to imagine their own animated film on the topic.

Think about music

- Some children need quiet to learn (and my generation were definitely supposed to work in silence).
- Others work better to music – it's just important to think about appropriate background music rather than something distracting.
- Try using rhythm and rhyme to learn material.
- Or even try setting a summary of what's being learned to music.

Some children work better with others

- Talk about what your child is trying to learn.
- Ask him or her to explain it to you. They could even act as the teacher and give you a lesson.
- Let them work with a friend or compare notes.

If your child finds it hard to sit still, try to involve them physically in what they are learning:

- Distribute post-it notes around a room, or even the house, with key information written on each one.
- Write notes on cards and order them in a sequence.
- Make use of the computer to write questions and type in the answers.
- Talk through information while you are walking or on a journey.

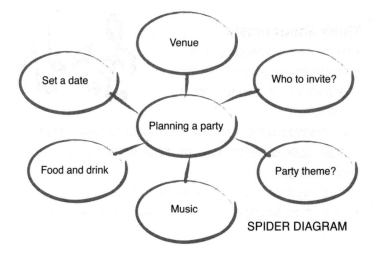

SPIDER DIAGRAM

Spider Diagrams and Mind Maps

Spider diagrams and mind maps can be very useful in all sorts of ways. Students find them particularly helpful for:

- Note-taking in lessons.
- Revising.
- Planning a piece of work, whether a letter, story, short essay, or a longer project.
- Brainstorming.

They can be applied to any subject. The idea of spider diagrams has been around for a while but educational consultant Tony Buzan improved on them in his books on mind-mapping by adding colour, keywords and pictures.

- Both link ideas and information.
- They work visually to help memory and prompt ideas.
- A central image represents the main subject.
- Thick coloured lines radiate from the centre for each of the most important points on the topic.

- Extra branches fill in the detail on each point.
- Pictures can be added.
- Key words are underlined.
- Colour is used to represent different strands of thought.

Many children find spider diagrams and mind maps a useful addition to their learning tools, helping them organize information and think more clearly about a subject.

Final word

Try to make sure your children enjoy what they learn – at least some of the time. I hope this book has changed your attitude towards their homework so that, whatever the subject, you can approach it with confidence, knowing that you really can help.

'That is what learning is. You suddenly understand something you've understood all your life, but in a new way.'
DORIS LESSING

INDEX